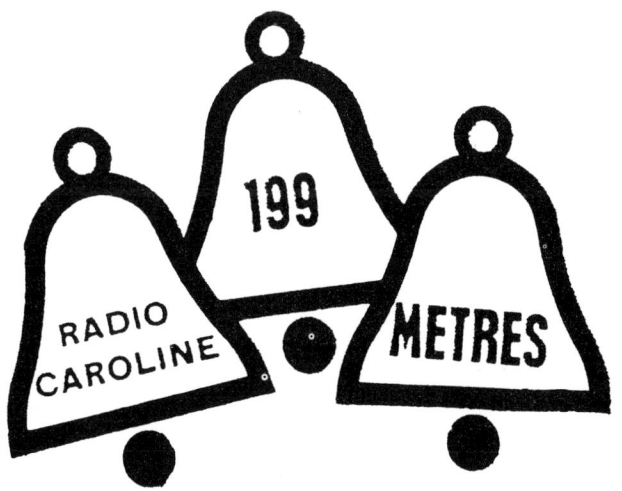

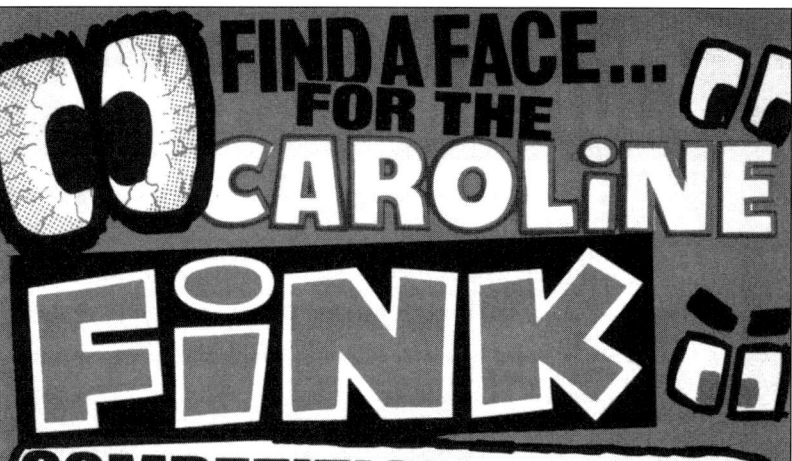

FIND A FACE... FOR THE CAROLINE FINK
COMPETITION IT'S FREE

CAROLINE CLUB · CAROLINE CLUB

THINK 'FINK'

TAKE YOUR PICK FROM ANY ONE OF 1,000 FABULOUS QUALITY PRIZES. THIS IS ALL YOU HAVE TO DO.

Just give us your idea of what you think a really way-out 'FINK' should look like. Anything goes. You can draw him (or her or it?) yourself, cut out pieces from magazines and stick them down or cut out some of the examples given inside this folder and draw round them or paint, nail, rivet or bolt down what you think is the most original idea for our Caroline 'FINK'. Anythink goes so start FINKING!!

When you've finished your 'FINK' turn the page, fill in all sections clearly and cut along dotted line.

DON'T FORGET TO MARK YOUR **CHOICE** OF PRIZES AS YOU MIGHT WELL BE ONE OF 1,000 LUCKY WINNERS! AND ALSO GIVE YOUR CAROLINE CLUB MEMBERSHIP NUMBER.

REMEMBER - NEATNESS WILL COUNT.

Rockin' and Rollin' with

The legendary radio station from beginning to end

On-Air 1964 - 1968

BOB PREEDY

A Broadcasting History book
published by
R.E.Preedy
Wetherby LS22 6WG

Copyright 2004
ISBN 1-874366-04-7

All rights reserved
No reproduction in any form unless with written
permission from the publisher

Printed in the UK by Amadeus Press, Cleckheaton

Photographs used in this book have come from many sources over
the years. It is impossible to name all the original photographers.
If any copyright has been infringed, this will be corrected in the
next edition.

CONTENTS

INTRODUCTION

CHAPTER ONE *RADIO CAROLINE SETS SAIL - FROM GREENORE & BACK*

CHAPTER TWO *THE MANX REACTION*

CHAPTER THREE *RADIO CAROLINE NORTH - ON THE AIR*

CHAPTER FOUR *THE BEAUTIFUL ISLE OF MAN*

CHAPTER FIVE *LIFE AFTER THE MOA - THE FINAL SIX MONTHS*

ACKNOWLEDGEMENTS

RIP

POSTSCRIPT

RECOMMENDED READING

RADIO 270 UPDATE

INTRODUCTION

This year - four decades after the launch of Radios Caroline and Atlanta, the interest in offshore radio remains just as strong. The sound from the sea still feels exciting in a way that legal commercial stations have never achieved. Also forty years ago the Labour government began its campaign to ban the stations. Ministers described the pirates as "fly by night companies" transmitting "low brow programmes for the ill educated masses".

In Prime Minister Harold Wilson's 800 page memoirs, "The Labour Government 1964 - 1970 A Personal Record", pirate radio merits just one paragraph -

"A campaign developed against the Government's decision to clamp down on the maritime pirate radios, adding a new and youthful element to the demonstrators I had to face whenever I went about the country."

In the same book the constitutional crisis on the Isle of Man caused by the

Introduction

imposition of the Marine Offences Act - "an unjust law from the mainland" - receives no mention at all.

The published diaries of Tony Benn show a divided cabinet on the subject. Benn suggested commercials on the BBC Light Programme - he also raised fundamental questions like, "Are we making the most of radio and TV in this country? Is public service synonymous with monopoly and is advertising synonymous with commercial broadcasting?" His cabinet colleague Richard Crossman advocated no action against the pirates until a satisfactory substitute radio service was offered nationwide.

While the future of offshore radio was of great concern to listeners, it generated little interest at the heart of government. Equally there is no mention in Edward Heath's memoirs of a secret and intriguing meeting he had with Phil Solomon just weeks before the 1966 General Election.

MEDIUM WAVE

Tune along the medium wave and there are dozens of stations offering music, news and conversation. During the evening hundreds more crowd in and any night it's possible to hear English broadcasts from the international services of Sweden, Holland, Belgium, China and Russia.

The reason we can hear the rest of the world is that night time AM Medium and Long Wave signals bounce off the ionosphere and travel further than their normal daytime ground waves. The downside of this extra distance is that the sky and ground signals can later combine to produce the phasing and fading affectionately associated with Radio Luxembourg.

Each country jealously guards its allocated frequencies and is loathe to hear foreign broadcasts interfering with their airspace. The allocation is negotiated by international conferences - the first was in 1926. The urgency for order in the ether was caused by the huge rise in radio stations and transmitters across a crowded Europe.

In 1948, 620 European transmitters had a combined power of 20 million watts. By 1976, 1450 masts broadcast with an output of 82 million watts. So while we enjoy the freedom to publish any written material, the right to broadcast is heavily regulated. The listener, though, is rarely consulted. Back in the sixties listeners neither demanded BBC local radio, nor wished for the removal of offshore radio.

In America the geography of the land allowed a freer system to flourish. Local radio was the only solution to broadcasting - transmitter technology wasn't developed enough to cover America with a national service with three time zones. By 1920 the stateside airwaves were crowded with pure

RADIO CAROLINE North

unrestricted commercial programming.

Europe at this time was still in an age of experimentation. The first wireless "programme", a musical concert, came from the Hague in Holland on the 6th November 1919. This received an enthusiastic welcome in the UK and two years later an appeal for funds to continue the project raised £750 in the UK alone.

By 1922 the Marconi company commenced an experimental service for London, with the call sign 2LO. A few months later, with encouragement from the GPO, six wireless manufacturers formed the British Broadcasting Company - by then a licence fee of ten shillings a years was required for every crystal set. In the next few years local stations were introduced producing their own distinctive service - as well as taking national news and talks programmes from London. One of them was 2LS in Leeds and Bradford from 1924. Very soon they were producing pioneering shows including a Palm Court Orchestra concert live from Scarborough. 2LS also began schools programmes, and made intricate live dramas, one involving actors down a coal pit inter-cut with a documentary about the mines.

A feeling from London that the local stations were becoming too popular - and an improvement in transmitter technology - led to the new regional services in the early 30s. In 1925, a new National Service on 1600 metres LW had created more well produced and better-financed programmes and this also led to the demise of early local radio.

But the BBC monopoly didn't last long. Radio Paris put out a sponsored English programme in 1925 and the following year Radio Normandy started broadcasting to the south of England. Finally in the spring of 1933 Radio Luxembourg began its Europe wide broadcasts on 1250 LW. British listeners rapidly rejected the formal style of the BBC for a nightly Luxembourg schedule including the Kraft Cheese Music Hall of Fame, the Bile Beans Concert, the Andrews' Liver Salts Concert and of course the Ovaltineys Club - which by 1938 had a million UK members. In that year Radio Luxembourg held an 80% share of all UK listening. The BBC naturally complained and amazingly the government forced newspapers to cease publishing the Luxembourg schedule.

The popularity of Luxembourg programmes sparked a British proposal to establish a similar service from a station in Germany. In Britain the advertising industry had, in three years, quadrupled its business. By 1938 it was worth £1,700,000 and the industry was eager to find new outlets.

Introduction

GERMANY CALLING

In 1937 planning began on an ambitious scheme to encircle the UK with a number of transmitters carrying the same commercial broadcast. A company, Air Time Ltd, was secretly founded by Peter Eckersley on behalf of Oswald Mosley, head of the British Union of Fascists, and Bill Allen, head of the outdoor posters group and a one time operative with MI5. Mosley himself invested £100,000 and money was also thought to come from the head of the Italian Fascist party, Mussolini.

The idea was to cover the whole of Britain with three transmitters - one in Ireland, one on the island of Sark, and one from Germany. Mosley wanted the stations to generate revenue for his Fascist Party - and to "provide the people with an entertaining alternative to the dreary schoolmasters at the BBC." This, he added reassuringly, was not to be a propaganda station.

The technical expert in charge of the project was Peter Eckersley, former chief engineer of the BBC. In addition to being a director of Air Time Ltd, he also formed Radio Variety Ltd to sell advertising and programmes on the station. A medium wave frequency was offered (formerly used by the Polish Kattowitz service) and a transmitter site chosen at Osterloog, near Norddeich in North West Germany. The profits from the station were to be split 45% to Air Time Ltd, and 55% to an independent German company (the same proportion as between Radio Normandy and the French authorities.) By the spring of 1937 a thirty-year broadcast agreement had also been agreed with the Dame of Sark. Her son, Colin Beaumont, was a member of Mosley's inner circle.

To further the project, almost complete by 1939, Mosley's wife, Diana, made personal contact with Hitler who supported the project. However after many months of negotiations the proposal failed because of objections from the German military authorities.

The war of course curtailed the project and ended yet one more plan to break the monopoly of the BBC. Mosley was denied his ambition of being "the first revolutionary in history to conduct a revolution and at the same time to make the fortune which assured its success." The German transmitter site was later used to relay Radio Berlin with Lord Haw Haw to the UK and is still in use as "Bremen 1".

The war also eclipsed Luxembourg when the station was taken over by the German army and used for propaganda programmes. The station returned to normal English broadcasting on LW in 1945 and transferred to 208 MW in 1951. It became so successful that by the mid 50s all its airtime was block booked by record companies.

Offshore radio in the 60's. Radio Caroline encouraged other projects, like the Yorkshire station Radio 270

RADIO CAROLINE North

The mighty 208 transmitter built at Marnach in 1950

OFFSHORE RADIO

Meanwhile the BBC remained stuck in its wartime time warp with shows like "Music While You Work" and "Housewives Choice". For a small record company or publisher, it was impossible to find airtime for new artists and thoughts turned to the airwaves beyond the three-mile limit.

In 1955 the controller of the Light Programme, Kenneth Adam, was given the urgent task of formulating new ideas to counteract the drift to Radio Luxembourg " the enemy across the channel." His plans were certainly helped by the decision of the giant J.Walter Thompson advertising agency which advised clients to switch from Luxembourg to commercial TV.

From this complex mix of restrictions offshore radio was born. Plans for seaborne stations had been discussed from the 1930s. In 1958 Denmark became the first country in Europe to enjoy unrestricted broadcasts from Radio Mercur. The idea travelled down the coast to Holland in 1960 with the birth of Veronica and from 1961 Radio Nord's broadcasts to Sweden. This was so successful a second Danish station DCR commenced in September 1961. It could only be a matter of time before entrepreneurs in Britain would try to break the broadcasting monopoly.

Bob Preedy
Wetherby
March 2004

CHAPTER ONE

RADIO CAROLINE SETS SAIL - FROM GREENORE & BACK

In 1962 music publisher and entrepreneur Allan Crawford was as frustrated with the radio service as were the new generation of listeners. The BBC was still stuck in wartime mode - with few programmes catering for teenagers.

A cultural trend had started in America during the mid 50s. The emergence of Rhythm and Blues and Rock and Roll for the jukebox market also made inroads into American commercial radio. Powerful stations in Mexico made unrestricted broadcasts to the southern states. Alan Freed was exposing the new 45s on his late night Moondog Rock'n' Roll Show. Package tours were travelling across America with up to ten new acts. Fading old cinemas and theatres were given a new lease of life as teenagers flocked to them to see and hear their new stars. The number of singles released each week was growing rapidly and from 1957 a new type of radio station cashed in on this exciting new sound.

First pioneered at Omaha's KOWH and then refined at WINS, New York and KLIF in Dallas, the top 40 format was based on the astute observation of jukebox customers who played the same songs over and over. Rock and Roll Radio thus became the sensation of the late 50s and early 60s.

The number of record releases increased dramatically in America but

RADIO CAROLINE North

not all made it to Britain. The "London American" label became the one to watch for its legendary roster. This Decca subsidiary licensed singles from a vast array of independent labels across America. Here in our record shops each week was the cream of the rock and roll era.

Entrepreneurs over here naturally searched out local talent to cover these gems - and this led to the emergence of not only a squad of Elvis, Gene and Eddie soundalikes but also a small coterie of very powerful and rich managers. Svengali figures like Larry Parnes, Reg Calvert, Larry Page and Gordon Mills signed up dozens of groups and sent them out on package tours into local ABC and Odeon Cinemas across the country.

The emerging wealth created by this enterprise was carefully controlled by a small number of star-makers working in conjunction with record companies to maximize profits.

Radio broadcasting from the BBC was slow to recognize the new audience for pop records - mainly because of the restrictions set up in the dance band era of the thirties and forties. The BBC had been obliged to enter into expensive deals to attract the bands away from their very lucrative tours of theatres and music halls during the depressed 1930s. Radio was seen as a great threat to this livelihood and many bandleaders were loathe to perform in a medium that would allow millions of listeners to hear their works without buying a theatre ticket. The BBC was also struggling for an audience against Radio Luxembourg where British restrictions did not apply. By competing the BBC was almost held to ransom by the musicians who demanded top remuneration as well as tough contract restrictions.

The record industry was also seen as a threat to live music and to stop the BBC from playing the 78s and not employing hundreds of musicians, the concept of "needle-time" was introduced. This meant that only a small amount of music could be broadcast from records. Of course this also suited the record companies and music publishers who only wanted a limited exposure of their product - they didn't want the consumer to stop buying records and sheet music.

With hindsight it was to prove a disaster for new independent artists who stood no chance of breaking through these restrictions. But back in the 30s it was the only way the BBC could regain its home audience from the twin threats of Radio Luxembourg and Radio Normandy. Both the BBC and the government made many attempts to curtail this airtime invasion, but listeners had the choice and wireless sets tuned defiantly to the continental stations.

FROM GREENORE & BACK

This attempt to control listening is a recurring theme from all governments. Europe might be a much different place if unrestricted listening over the ether had been encouraged. For instance the extreme ends of politics like communism and fascism, keenly debated in the 30s, are now rarely discussed - leaving us today hearing the view from a very narrow centre ground.

In 1946 the BBC reorganised its output along the lines of high, middle and lowbrow entertainment - the Third Programme of classical music, the Home Service with talks and discussion and the Light Programme to entertain the returning troops. The Light, the most popular service was still hidebound with the restrictions formulated a decade before and rarely gave a nod to the emerging music explosion of the 50s.

From the late 40s Country and Western was to prove a potent force in American radio. Artists like Hank Williams and Bob Wills brought a new exuberance to the airwaves and jukeboxes. The BBC Light Programme even featured a weekly recording of the Louisiana Hayride - a hugely popular live show featuring the cream of Country artists. Rock and Roll though was not to be heard on the BBC.

Happily Radio Luxembourg was more in tune with its audience and ran Alan Freed's seminal show. Airtime on Luxembourg was quickly snapped up by record companies who used their fifteen or thirty minute shows to spotlight all their new releases for the week. This curious mixture could vary from show tunes, crooning ballads to the raw sound of Eddie Cochran. And the time allotted for each disc was frequently less than a minute. Of course the record company wanted us to rush out the following morning to buy the whole song.

This then was the system that frustrated any new artist not on a major label. The owner of London's Scene Club, Ronan O'Rahilly, had a number of promising acts but both the BBC and Luxembourg thwarted his promotion efforts. When he heard about Australian Allan Crawford's bid to break this monopoly, he became an enthusiastic potential investor.

THE UK FLEET

Crawford, long ignored as the originator of 60s UK pirate radio, was aware of the offshore ships in Denmark and Sweden. As early as 1960 he was a shareholder in CBC (Plays) Ltd, with Kitty Black and Oliver Smedley. The company was described as "Commercial Radio agents" and they were fully aware of the efforts of governments to ban these broadcasts.

Radio Nord off the Swedish coast was set up following the success of

RADIO CAROLINE North

Denmark's Radio Mercur from July 1958. Radio Nord was backed by American money - most from the men behind KLIF, Dallas, one of the first Stateside Top 40 stations.

Off the coast of Holland from Easter 1960 was the legendary Radio Veronica - easily audible in the UK and totally different from the output of the Light Programme. The Music Box had been opened and Crawford made a bid for Radio Nord, outlawed by the Swedish government from the end of July 1962. This fully equipped radio station would need little conversion - she was equipped with two 10-kilowatt Continental MW transmitters and was also planning an FM service, but closed down on 30th June 1962 once negotiations with Allan Crawford were complete.

Crawford tried to gather finance for the station and it was all in place

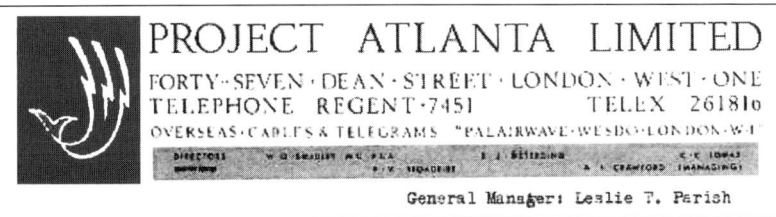

until 16th August when Danish police boarded and seized Radio Mercur. One of Crawford's major backers, John Delaney, pulled out of the enterprise. The Radio Nord boat sailed to Spain for refurbishment but by September was moored in the Thames estuary ready to start broadcasts. By now though the project was lacking finance and an offer to lease rather than buy the boat was refused. At Christmas 1962 the owners sent her back to Galveston where she was stripped of all radio equipment.

A year elapsed before fresh finance could be obtained to buy the £75,000 boat and during this hiatus Ronan O'Rahilly heard of the project and was invited in as a potential investor. With his connections in the City he realised that finance wasn't a problem and set about

also planning his own radio ship.

The MV Fredericia had been a passenger and car ferry working between Copenhagen and Malmo, Sweden. At the end of her service in 1963 she was sold to a Swedish company, Alraune and taken to Rotterdam where Planet Productions later inspected her. In a complex deal O'Rahilly took shares in Alraune, who then rented the boat to the

From September 1964, the new studio giving DJs self-operation of equipment.

Caroline group. This elegant ship then quietly slipped out of Holland bound for Ireland on 13th February 1964. Although planning for the radio ship had been kept secret, questions were raised in parliament about the legality of the enterprise, some seven days before she left Rotterdam.

The ship offered superior accommodation and working conditions. Her central lounge was still in the original 1930s style and from there a wide staircase with wooden banisters lead down to individual cabins.

RADIO STUDIO

The Radio Caroline North studio was later moved to the old sun lounge. Martin Kayne provides a detailed description.

RADIO CAROLINE North

The studio contained a small Gates mixer that had four or five channels. The first two rotary controls from the left were the DJ's microphone and next the news microphone which was bolted to a small desk on the other side of the studio. There were two push buttons (like on a doorbell also attached to the news desk so the newsreader could fire appropriate jingles by remote control. The second and third channels would control the output levels of all the other studio equipment, 2 Spotmaster cartridge players, 2 Gates transcription turntables with large Grey pick-ups, the tracking weight of each was increased by the attachment of 2 one penny coins above the stylus. Also 2 Ampex heavy-duty tape recorders, which had separate, play and record heads that enabled them to be used to create and echo effect. A row of switches in the middle of the mixer enabled the operator to select which of the two channels would carry the audio from the selected items. The up position gave you channel 3, middle position was off, and down position was channel 4. This could be confusing when attempting to use many items almost simultaneously, so many DJ had several switches in both the up and down position, meaning that more than one item of equipment was sharing the same level control. The knob on the far right was a master control which seldom required any movement.

Studio desk

Above the panel was a book rest with a clipboard containing items to be read, or instructions for the days broadcasting and a programme schedule.

Two red pigmy bulbs on this warned when a microphone was open.

The DJ's microphone was the square type of AKG that were in common use at the time and was supported by a metal stand rather than the anglepoise device. Two loudspeakers behind the DJ monitored the sound and a headphone socket was to the left of the panel.

The record library was outside the studio that had been constructed on the after-deck, it had previously been below next to the transmitter room. The library also housed the newsroom in which a radio receiver, typewriter and another Ampex recorder stood. There was also a spare turntable and amplifier so DJ's

FROM GREENORE & BACK

could listen to records outside the studio. Another interesting point was that the record library was always warm as there was a ventilation hatch which could be opened allowing hot air from the forced air transmitter cooling system to enter the room: A shirt could be washed...and dry before the end of your show. Also in the record library was a cage that contained the RF combiner that allowed both of the 10kW transmitters to be run together to hopefully produce 20kW.

The transmitter room was on deck level, more or less below the studio where the two Continental Electronics transmitters stood side by side along with an audio compressor/limiter. This room also served as a workshop and contained much electrical test equipment and spare components. The transmitters each contained a series of safety features which would cause them to shut down in the event of a problem. In very rough weather

Record Library

Continental transmitter

RADIO CAROLINE North

it was not uncommon for them to switch off, seldom both together, but the engineer would have to be on hand to push the reset button. I am not sure if this was due to the transmitters being tilted and tossed around or the effects of the waves breaking over the aerial upsetting the antenna tuning.

2 Mercedes generators provided power during broadcasting hours, after which a ships generator took over and supplied both the ship and the studios. If you were doing any meaningful production after broadcasting time it was worth checking with the ships engineer that the alternating current provided for the studio was at 50 c.p.s. or you could find all your recordings being either fast or possibly slow when played back with the main generator running.

The ships engine was run every Monday and the bilges pumped as the old ship leaked a bit through the propeller shaft. We did have a practice abandon ship as part of an emergency drill conducted by a Dutch captain. We had self-inflating life rafts which was very fortunate...the wooden lifeboat when lowered over the side promptly sank!

The antenna was a folded dipole with a multiple wire forming one leg and the steel mast as the other. The loading coils were in a purpose built cupboard in the ships lounge with heavy duty coaxial cable leading to the transmitters. In fact the mess room monitor speaker was just an amplifier and speaker with a piece of wire just wrapped around this feeder cable. The tall mast was counterbalanced by very heavy slabs of old reinforced concrete from a demolished bridge placed in the ship's lower hold.

The MV Caroline/Fredericia had been a passenger ferry so the DJ's had excellent living quarters with a washbasin and electric heater in each cabin. Portholes with curtains and a wide staircase similar to that of a hotel leading upstairs to the main lounge and dining room.

Dining room

THE BATTLE TO BE FIRST

Allan Crawford's Project Atlanta had also raised sufficient finance to proceed and both groups worked in tandem to create their stations at the same port of Greenore in Ireland. The port was owned by O'Rahilly's father and

FROM GREENORE & BACK

Caroline starts a radio revolution

was sufficiently isolated and well away from officialdom.

Even though Crawford's ship had been planned well in advance, it was to be Caroline that was first to broadcast. Under the command of Captain Baeker she slipped out of Greenore on Tuesday 24th March after a hectic few weeks of installations and renovation. The nearest record shop, at Dundalk, had been cleared of its stock as the Caroline crew bought two copies of the Top 50 and many oldies albums. The ship arrived off Felixstowe late afternoon on Good Friday 27th March 1964 and made its first test transmission on 1495kHz (201m) around 7pm and continued on and off beyond midnight. The tests included a taped show by John Junkin. A longer transmission started Saturday at noon on 1520kHz (197m) with Jimmy McGriff's Round Midnight, followed by Simon Dee on tape saying *"This is Radio Caroline on 199, your all day music station. The time right now is one minute past twelve and that means it's time for Christopher Moore"* who then played "Not Fade Away" by the Rolling Stones.

Disappearing rapidly though was the ship's registration - reportedly withdrawn by Panama on 3rd April 1964 after pressure from the British government. This may have been misinformation leaked to the press as it appears Panama quietly ignored the request and the ship continued to fly the Panamanian flag for the rest of her commercial days.

RADIO CAROLINE North

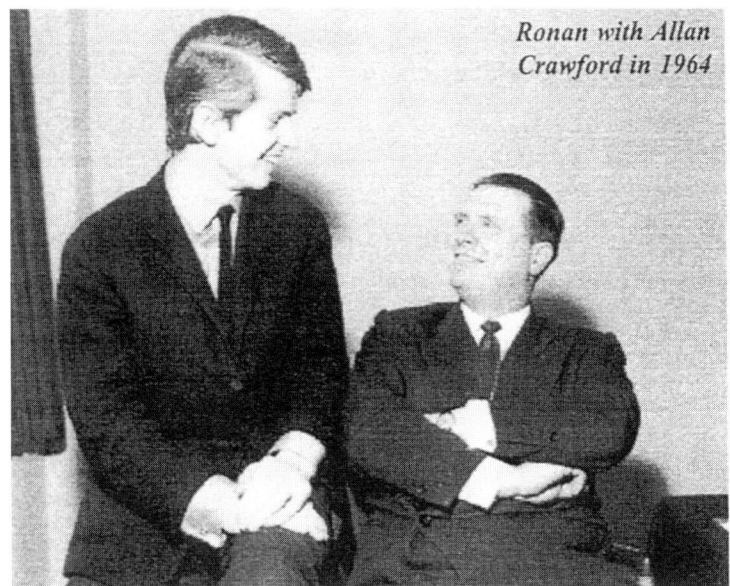

Two ships and two bosses - an uneasy alliance.

Allan Crawford's Radio Atlanta arrived a month later and began tests on 9th May. Regular shows started from 6pm on 12th May and mostly featured cover versions of the top songs on Crawford's own labels, Cannon, Sabre, Rocket and Carnival. He even released a cover of "Caroline" by the Caroliners on Sabre SA456 in 1964. However two ships side by side off the Essex coast competing for the same audience caused advertisers to hold back until a clear winner was established.

On 22nd June 1964 American Don Pierson read an article in the Wall Street Journal about the two UK offshore stations. He immediately flew to London where he tried to meet Ronan O'Rahilly who, not surprisingly, declined the offer. Undaunted, Pierson flew over the North Sea to see the ships. He returned to Texas determined to start his own high-powered station to be modelled on the successful American Top 40 format.

With this knowledge of looming competition O'Rahilly had to act fast. Advertisers were still cautious about offshore radio. A third station in the Thames estuary would be catastrophic for revenue. Alan Crawford, possibly unaware of the American backed station, entered merger talks with Radio Caroline. He had always wanted the lucrative London market and was now being offered what seemed like exclusivity in the South East.

NEWS RELEASE

COMMERCIAL RADIO MERGER

The directors of Project Atlanta and Planet Productions Limited today issued a joint statement announcing a merger between Radio Atlanta and Radio Caroline.

The companies are responsible for the advertising and selling of time on the two off-shore commercial radio stations.

Mr. Allan Crawford, Managing Director of Project Atlanta, and Mr. Ronan O'Rahilly, Managing Director of Planet Productions, will become joint managing directors of the new operation.

The ship broadcasting the present Radio Caroline programmes, m.v. Caroline, will sail to the Isle of Man tomorrow morning (Friday) to a position five miles from Ramsey, Isle of Man. It will continue to broadcast Radio Caroline programmes on the way to its destination and will remain on 199 metres medium wave.

The ship m.v. Atlanta will continue broadcasting from its present position to the Greater London area and South East England under the national call sign, Radio Caroline.

In their joint statement Mr. Crawford and Mr. O'Rahilly said:

"The decision to merge was taken in view of the enormous interest from the public and advertisers in other parts of England outside the original broadcasting area. This network will cover the most populous areas of Great Britain.

"It will specifically meet the demands from advertisers in the North and Midlands and from existing advertisers who are already taking time on the two stations.

"All departments will merge to operate from one office. The Caroline Club and other land-based operations will continue and be extended to cover the new broadcasting area".

RADIO CAROLINE North

The original plans were for the Caroline ship was to be moored in the north with a sales office in Liverpool. Now with little advertising on either ship, a merger was announced with Caroline taking over Atlanta's debts in return for a third of future profits. O'Rahilly's original Caroline would sail north and Radio Atlanta was renamed Caroline South. The two ships could now offer advertisers nationwide coverage - but behind the smiles was an unresolved and ultimately corrosive war between Crawford and O'Rahilly.

Both stations closed down on Friday 2nd July at 8pm and by midnight Radio Caroline was alongside Atlanta to unload a stock of pre-recorded programme tapes - produced months before in Radio Atlanta's Dean Street studios. Allan Crawford's boat was now renamed as Caroline South.

At 5.30am the following day Captain Abraham Hangerfeld followed his secret orders to take the original Radio Caroline to the north of England. On board and broadcasting as she sailed were two volunteer DJs, Tom Lodge and Jerry Leighton, plus sound desk operator Alan Turner. By Monday afternoon 5th July at 3pm the ship anchored off Maughold Head near Ramsey in the Isle of Man and was quickly circled by the coastguard cutter "Valiant". After a marathon journey around the coast of Britain, Radio Caroline had arrived with a mission to entertain the north.

Tom Lodge greets the Isle of Man

CHAPTER TWO

THE MANX REACTION

For a short time everyone on board the ship was apprehensive about the new surroundings. Why was there no flotilla of small boats to welcome them? Where were the customary flashing lights from cars that had followed them around the south coast? Perhaps new competition for the fledgling Manx Radio had soured relations even before Caroline had been introduced to the island. An ominous silence had greeted the radio ship - except for one brave gesture. Two people on a canoe had paddled from Ramsey out to the ship to hand over an envelope containing the words - Welcome to the Isle of Man.

From then on the ice was broken. The station's arrival created headlines and within a few days Radio Caroline North was forging lasting friendships. Captain Hangerfeld made a broadcast saying they were not coming to disturb the peace of the Isle of Man but hoped to make many friends here. DJs aboard the ship praised the island's scenery and mentioned about the car lights and mirrors and asked if anyone would care to show their presence. Many showed they had already tuned in. As it was Tynwald Day, all government offices were closed, so there was no official reaction, but some people did question why Manx Radio could only transmit with very low power while a new radio ship could cover the whole of the north.

The next day, Tuesday, two officials met the press. Mr V Weijsmuller and Mr J C Focke from the Offshore Tender and Supply Co. said from their base at the Mitre Hotel how they were busy organising fuel, food and water supplies.

Meanwhile a wave of pop music burst over the island daily from 6am to 9pm and then again from midnight to 3am - the three-hour break because of severe interference on the waveband. A massive coverage area was predicted with good reception expected across the whole of the north of England, southern Scotland, Ireland, north Wales and the north Midlands. Fan mail began to arrive within days confirming excellent daytime reception.

Very shortly a notice was displayed in the office of the Ramsey Harbour Masters - destined to complicate life for the radio ship.

RADIO CAROLINE North

Any vessel visiting the radio ship Caroline or any other similar ship is required to obtain customs clearance outwards and must also report inwards on return. Cargo taken to such radio ship is subject to export control, including export licensing control.
HM CUSTOMS AND EXCISE.

On Wednesday 15th July the Caroline skipper, the chief engineer and liaison officer were brought from the ship into Ramsey on Alf Duggan's pleasure cruiser, the Lucille. Also joining the team was a new recruit to the DJ team Tony Jay who had flown into Ronaldsway that morning. They were all in Ramsey to greet the press and take them back for a viewing of the radio ship. The following day the island learnt about its new neighbours:

"47 year old Captain Hangerfeld, married with one daughter, was employed by the Offshore Tender Co in Baarn, Holland. His normal job is to deliver ships all over the world. Once Caroline is secure at her anchor he would hand over in August to a new captain. After that his next assignment was to deliver a trawler to Mexico. One problem on board is the storage of water. Usage of about one ton per day meant a twice-weekly trip by the trawler, the Essex Girl to refill the capacity of 70 tons.
The Swedish Chief Engineer, Mr Ove Sjostrom detailed the on-board allowances - 2 tins of beer and one Coke a day and 200 cigarettes a week.
For Tony Jay, 25, an ex-school teacher from Swansea, this was his first job as a DJ and he will provide two weeks of holiday and leave cover for the other presenters. Technical operator, Paul LeMare, 29, from Harrow, used to work for ABC TV, and his job is to play in the records, tapes, jingles and commercials for the DJs."

On Thursday 9th July the Caroline liaison officer, 28 year old, George Hare flew in from Dublin and gave details of Caroline's advertising rates. Advertisers were already requesting space - on the first weekend, 11th July, an ad campaign had been booked by the News of the World.

ADVERTISING

The rates on Caroline North offered by Planet Productions Ltd, Dawson Street, Dublin were 6am to 7am £32 per minute, 30 secs £16 and 7 secs £7. The breakfast rate from 7am would be £60 for one minute. Between 9am and midday - considered the peak hours, one minute £80,

30 secs £40 and 7 secs £17. From midday the rates dropped to £66 per minute. From 3pm to 4.30pm one minute was £46, rising from 4.30 to 6pm to £66. Discounts were offered of 5% for 26 spots and 15% for 79 and over.

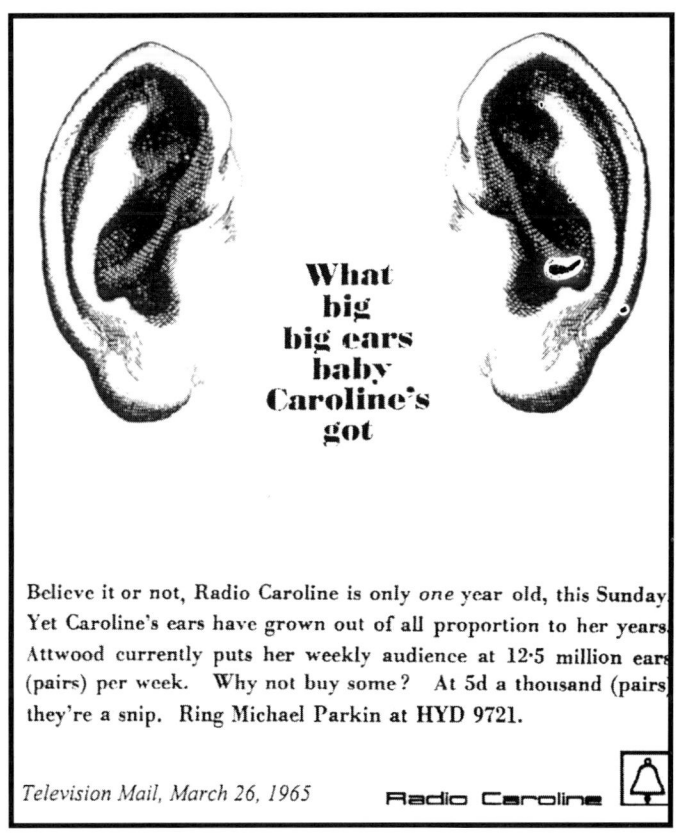

What big big ears baby Caroline's got

Believe it or not, Radio Caroline is only *one* year old, this Sunday. Yet Caroline's ears have grown out of all proportion to her years. Attwood currently puts her weekly audience at 12·5 million ears (pairs) per week. Why not buy some? At 5d a thousand (pairs) they're a snip. Ring Michael Parkin at HYD 9721.

Television Mail, March 26, 1965   Radio Caroline

Before taking a boat to Caroline, George Hare stopped off at Blakemore's record shop in Victoria Street, Douglas to pick up the latest Top 50 entries. Later that day he also met with Bernard Swales, Manager of the Ramsey Steamship Company, and Mrs D M Quayle JP, Chairman of the Ramsey Commissioners.

Meanwhile the embattled Manx Radio saw a slump in both listeners and advertising revenue. The British government again refused to allow the station a medium wave frequency. John Grierson, manager of Manx Radio said, *"I feel that they are condoning radio piracy"*. The GPO had no proposals to take action against Caroline and in fact gave the station

Above: Manx Radio's first studio.

Left: Caroline car pendant.

RADIO CAROLINE North

a special box number at the Ramsey Post Office. Manx Radio meanwhile continued to be heard only on VHF.

THE MANX REACTION

Pop groups appearing on the island were quick to appreciate the publicity value of being heard on Caroline. The Dave Clark Five were some of the first visiting stars in July.

Freddie and Dreamers planned a trip on Monday 27th July, but were unable to make the journey because of bad weather.

Dave Clark in the studio

RADIO CAROLINE North

A new technical operator joined the Ship at the end of July, 19 year old David Turner, former leader of the Jaunters beat group. He was to spend two weeks out of three on board organising the play list and spinning in the discs for the DJs. (His son, Juan, now runs Energy FM on the island)

TENSION

On the South ship, hints of the future began to emerge. Tony Blackburn joined in July 1964, and saw the bitter arguments at Head Office between Joint MD's Allan Crawford and Ronan O'Rahilly. *"Allan gave me my job of Caroline South and there was not an ounce of malice in him. He was charming to me and probably was a bit too nice to deal with some of the mafia and bouncer-types around Ronan".*
Later after Phil Solomon joined the organisation, Blackburn was tested to see if he'd take a bribe to play a song. He was offered £20 to play a Bachelors track on the breakfast show - an offer he refused.
After Christmas 1964 Caroline South's audience slumped against the competition from Radio London. An audience survey at the time gave Caroline South only 0.9%, Radio London 14% and the BBC Light Programme 30%. Caroline North was soon taking twice as much in advertising revenue as her sister ship. In February 1965 the BBC Light Programme responded to the competition by increasing its sound compression from 6db (used since February 1961) to 12db to give the station a punchier, more "pirate" sound.
Simon Dee also lifted the lid on the power struggles inside the secret world of offshore radio. The uneasy relationship in the boardroom was a cause for much concern on the boats. The popularity of the stations had taken everyone by surprise. Head Office became top heavy and displayed an arrogant attitude to the broadcasting crew on the boats. *"Those sitting comfortably and warm in Chesterfield Gardens very quickly showed little interest in our well being out in the North Sea. We were enduring appalling weather conditions and somehow expected a pat on the back once in a while. It never came".*
While on shore leave, Simon Dee would call in at Head Office, but often felt a bystander. All around he saw sharp operators doing deals and making a small fortune. Back on the boats the DJs who created the shows, only earned £20 a week. *"With two captains a ship hasn't a chance of steering a straight course. While I was with Caroline power games raged as the two factions in the administration fought for supremacy".*

CHAPTER THREE

RADIO CAROLINE NORTH - ON THE AIR
1964-1968

"Pirate Radio? Impoverished programmes for the ill-educated masses"
Quote by Labour MP Christopher Reynolds 15 February 1967.

In spite of the above description of the stations, an audience survey carried out between 25th August and 13th September 1964 gave an indication of Caroline's huge popularity. The survey was commissioned before the arrival of Radio London, which subsequently decimated the audience for Caroline South.

The audience for Radio Caroline North in any one day amounted to 3,916,000 listeners. The peak listening period Monday to Friday was between 12.30 and 1pm when 1,404,000 were tuned to 199. Over the weekend the audience increased with the Saturday peak between 12 and 1pm at 1,449,000. Sunday from 11.30 to midday was even higher at 1,889,000. The home audience was not surprisingly slightly more women than men, and comprised more than twice the number of 35 plus age group than 16 - 24 year olds. The listeners were also more active containing more cinemagoers than ITV viewers.

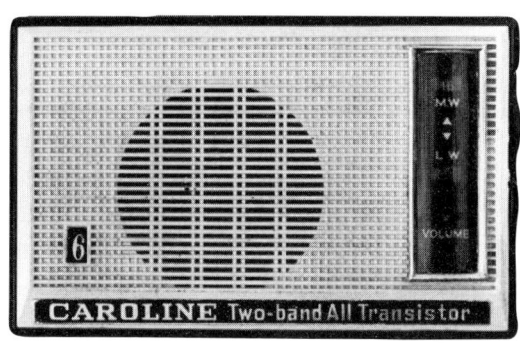

RADIO CAROLINE North

SOUNDING FINE ON 199

1964

Tom Lodge

Jerry Leighton

For the first month of broadcasting Tom Lodge and Jerry Leighton alternated shows - with Alan Turner presenting the midday "Date with Caroline", the 6pm "Sunset Spin" and the midnight "Late, Late Show." Tony Jay arrived on Wednesday 15th July and soon hosted the 2pm "Soundtrack" show and the "Late Show." His stay on the ship continued until Monday 14th September - his final show being "Downbeat" from 7 to 9pm.

Roger Gale who presented his first show on the afternoon of August Bank

ON THE AIR 1964-1968

Holiday Monday, returned from leave on Tuesday 15th September and replaced pop star and Coronation Street actor Chris Sandford who had joined the station mid-August. From Saturday 12th September there was no Midnight show for two weeks due to engineering maintenance on the aerial and transmitter.

Also that month the studio was relocated from deck level to the top deck in the cabin/lounge behind the ship's funnel. Even the ship's cook helped with the cabling and soldering so the studio would be ready for the next morning's breakfast show. From this point all the shows became self-op with the DJs operating the equipment themselves rather than giving hand signals to a technical operator.

If a DJ was not up to standard there was a traditional pirate method of terminating employment. The Programme Director would send a sealed letter via the tender to the captain, and the unfortunate DJ would be informed of the decision once he had landed on shore. Luckily most found new work almost immediately.

Roger Gale was "let go" by Chris Moore but was asked by Simon Dee and Ken Evans to join Caroline South in October for a period of three months. Stepping aboard the North ship were Caroline South DJs Errol Bruce, Mike Marriot and Bob Stewart (after only four weeks on air). A few weeks later Errol transferred back to the South ship and Mike Marriot left completely.

Bob Stewart

Bob Stewart later hosted a Caroline night at the Queen's Showbar, Cleveleys. Another haunt of Caroline DJs on shore leave was the Winmarith Club in Lytham Road, Blackpool. The club later expanded and was renamed the Lemon Tree Club in the Squires Gate Hotel. Both clubs were run by

RADIO CAROLINE North

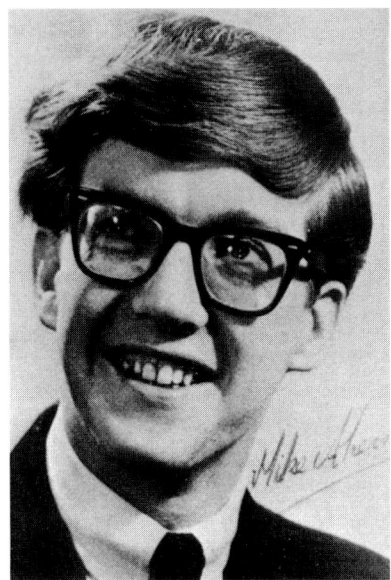

Mike Ahern

Sydney Levine, whose son Ian became a DJ/ promoter/record producer on the Northern Soul scene.
Joining the station in November were Ric Johns and Mike Ahern (a speaker of five foreign languages learnt during his two years as a grape picker).

1965

At the beginning of 1965 Jerry Leighton left to work at Caroline House in London. By March his slot was taken by Bill Hearne - now Programme Director of the North ship, replacing Chris Moore who had been in that position, in London, since the start. Also at that time Tom Lodge was the Senior DJ.

On the engineering side a young Australian, John Roberts, took a job on Caroline North. He had been working for Lab Gear and Pye in Cambridge but was bitten by the sense of adventure offered by offshore stations. During his time onboard he observed how Ronan O'Rahilly was unable to trust anyone - and John also clashed with the chief engineer, who he perceived as a bit of a conman. John's stay on the northern ship was for two months before transferring to the Southern boat - at the time in dry dock in Zanndam after being grounded at Frinton-On-Sea after atrocious weather on 21st January 1966. During this time John helped install a new 50kw transmitter. His next career move was to Swinging Radio England/Britain Radio on the Laissez Faire and finally John completed the hat trick by working on Radio London. He now runs his own MOR FM station in the North East tip of Australia.

In the summer of 65 Big Jim Murphy joined and hosted the 3 to 6pm slot as well as the

Jim Murphy

ON THE AIR 1964-1968

Two sea-dogs face to face

IT'S a terrifying moment for both man and dog. Disc jockey Jimmy Savile, looking as though he's dressed in mod "gear" rejects, prepares to leap aboard Radio Caroline.

Caroline's dog stands firm on the deck of the pirate radio ship anchored off the Isle of Man determined to repel all boarders.

With six feet between the two, the odds appear to be in favour of the dog.

But in the end the sea-dog Savile triumphed. Jimmy did not even get his life-jacket wet. And he tells the full story in true nautical style on page 13

Jimmy Savile

'Pirates took me prisoner'

SO, anyway, here I was in the Isle of Man for the week, as the Governor of a big beat comp, and what a week it turned out to be.

When you drive in from the airport you pass over a little humpback bridge where the Little People live. These Little People are Very Important Fairies. And you must shout "Hello Little People" as you pass. This makes everything O.K.!

With the backing of the Little People, I decided that if I could force my way the Radio Caroline and capture it, I could sail it to Liverpool and sell it as a high seas prize. So on Wednesday, disguised as a fisherman, I chartered a fast boat, the Essex Girl, and sailed for Caroline.

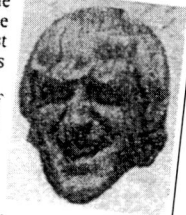

SURRENDER

By the time I got to Caroline we were going up and down like a loony lift and I was feeling decidedly off-side.

"Do you surrender?" I croaked into the wind.

"Hello Jimmy," shouted the sailor-type Disc jockeys. "Come aboard, if you can jump it."

Now, folks, you want to try jumping off the deck of a small, tossing boat on to the deck of a big unmoving boat with a big-foot gap of angry, boiling sea in between...

A jump of the legs and a sinking of the heart and there I was in a heap on the other deck, with the Caroline dog turning me over with his nose to see if I was fit to eat.

Anyway, I decided to surrender to them, and they treated me very fair as a prisoner. They even let me play a few discs on the air (Beatles, Stones, Elvis, Sonny and Cher, and my favourite-of-the-moment Beach Boys).

To be a floating disc jockey is to earn money the hard way, but it's a great experience to start, if any of you young guys can get in.

We land-based D.Js don't know we're born, except me as I was never so pleased to see that marvellous land as when I eventually got back.

RADIO CAROLINE North

highly popular Midnight Surf Party. He also created a Country and Western show, Saturday from 8.30 to 10pm. A syndicated show from WMCA's Jack Spector was aired on both stations from 7 to 8pm and also that summer American religious programmes commenced. "The Voice of Prophecy" ran from 7.55 to 8am with the more substantial "The World Tomorrow" airing from 8 to 8.30pm. On Sunday the 8pm "Radio Bible Class" was followed at 9 by Edward Hoffman. All these taped shows produced much needed revenue.

The summer relief DJ in 65 was 19-year-old Ray Teret from Manchester - who told the station he had experience in a ballroom/disco; he omitted to say it was as a waiter rather than a DJ! Also that summer, in July, a surprise visitor to the station was Jimmy Savile - who was helping out with a swimming marathon. The swimmers had to race out to the ship and back again - a pretty tough challenge. Jimmy Savile was invited aboard and played his favourite discs like the Beatles, Stones, Elvis, Sonny and Cher and the Beach Boys, during the lunch show.

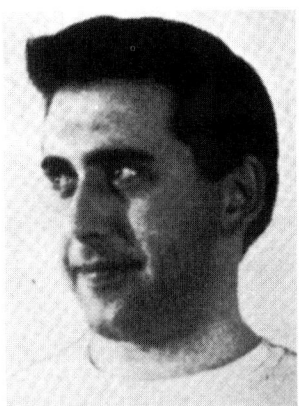

In the autumn of 1965, Don Allen joined. He had previously been on Caroline South and then spent some time at Caroline House. He replaced Tom Lodge, who was asked by Ronan O'Rahilly to take control of the southern ship then losing out heavily to the competition from Radio London. A survey showed that Caroline South had one seventh of London's audience.

Don Allen

In late November Tony Prince joined, at the same time as Mike Ahern left for a short time before returning. Bob Stewart was now Senior DJ.

The Ramsey lifeboat was called out at 2.30am on 22nd December 1965 and requested to bring a doctor to deal with an incident on the ship. The Captain had been

Tony Prince

bitten by a dog and needed eight stitches in his hand. The lifeboat, the Thomas Corbett, returned to base by 4.25am.

Tony Prince went south to help on Caroline's replacement ship, Cheetah II but then returned north as Mike Ahern went south to help re-establish an audience on Caroline South.

1966

CRAWFORD FORCED OUT - SOLOMON CALLED IN

It was at this time that urgent finance was required to sustain the business - to pay for urgent repairs and build up revenue for the ailing Caroline South. In December 1965 Planet Productions had acquired the assets of the virtually bankrupt Project Atlanta. Allan Crawford was voted off the board but remained at head office for a few months selling airtime. He had lost about £30,000 and was forced to sell his music catalogue to the Beatles' Northern Songs Ltd. From then until 1973 he produced budget tracks for the Pickwick label's "Top of the Pops" albums, before returning to Australia as head of Festival Records.

Phillip Solomon

Very quickly Ronan O'Rahilly approached impresario Philip Solomon to join the board. Solomon told me his investment amounted to £500,000 giving him 50% share and the dominant voice. What he found was an unfocussed group with little idea of financial control. As soon as money was earned it was as quickly spent with no thought to the long term. To finance this new venture he sold off a number of music publishing concerns to Ed Kassner and the Carlin music group.

Solomon was no stranger to record promotion. His father, Morris, had been a major distributor of records in Ireland since the fifties. He also had shares in Decca records. Philip and his brother Mervyn joined the family business and learned the inside working of the music world.

The life and death of Caroline. Busy and fun times on Ramsey Bay and a sad end in Amsterdam.

RADIO CAROLINE North

Philip's first solo project was as manager of Ruby Murray. Her phenomenal success commenced with the first six singles gracing the Top 10 in 1955.

Philip and his wife, Dorothy, moved from Dublin to London in 1958 and within two years had built up a hugely profitable vertical business, handling record production, music publishing and management. In 1963 brother Mervyn, who ran a chain of Irish record stores and a record label, was presented with a tape of a new group, Them - headed by lead singer Van Morrison. Such was the local success of Them, that a visit by Decca A& R man, Dick Rowe was arranged. Rowe had recently turned down the Beatles and was in a receptive mood to discover another R'n'B outfit. He agreed to sign the band on condition that Philip Solomon was their manager - he had proved his skills that same year by master minding 16 year old Twinkle's Decca smash hit, "Terry". Solomon's earlier success on Decca had been with the Bachelors from 1962 - their first hit, "Charmaine" was produced by Shel Talmy who later worked with the Who and the Kinks..

By agreeing to this managerial condition for Them in 1964, a battle of wills was inevitable between the mercurial Morrison and the iron willed Solomon. The band's first single, "Don't Start Crying Now", however made no impact. Their second track had to make it, and to ensure success, Solomon brought in legendary New York producer Bert Berns to re-record some previous tracks. One of these, "Baby Please Don't Go", featuring Jimmy Page on lead guitar, was adopted as a theme tune on the influential TV show, "Ready Steady Go".

Dorothy Solomon used her relationship with TV producers to place Them on the show - helped by the judgement of RSG trainee researcher and talent spotter, Joan Thirkettle - later to reappear in Solomon's radio empire.

By January 1965 Them were Top 10 with "Baby Please Don't Go" - with "Gloria" on the B-side. Their next single, "Here Comes the Night", with Andy White (session musician on early Beatle tracks) on drums, shot to No 2 in March 1965 - but was to be their final chart entry. Internal tension within the group and between their manager led to an uneasy year, at the end of which Solomon looked for an easier option. His decision to join Radio Caroline was prompted by his firm belief in record promotion.

HYPING THE CHARTS

John Repsche's fascinating book about the life and times of the legendary record producer, Joe Meek, reveals the hidden side of record promotion on radio. In 1954 Meek was a freelance sound engineer on the Radio Luxembourg Road Shows. He travelled around the UK recording such shows as This is Your Life, Strike It Rich, Candid Microphone and a forerunner of Opportunity Knocks, When You're Smiling.

LUXEMBOURG
7.30 Radio Reveille Reguests. 7.45 Explosive Sounds. 8.0 The Alan Freeman Show. 8.15 It's Pop Pye Time. 8.30 Pop Parade. 8.45 Radio Bingo Show. 9.0 David Jacobs' Startime. 9.30 A Date With Cathy. 9.45 New Tomorrow. 10.0 The Jimmy Young Hour. 11.0 Brian Matthew's Pop Parade. 11.15 Jimmy Savile's "15". 11.30 Pops Till Midnight. 12.0 Pops Past Midnight. 12.30 The Baron's Music In The Night. 3 a.m. Close down.

The Luxembourg schedule on August 14th 1967.

A decade later to obtain airplay on Luxembourg, Meek placed many of his songs with a subsidiary of publishers, Campbell Connelly. Ivy Music was co-owned with Radio Luxembourg, so the more Ivy published songs played, the more royalties accrued for the station. When this deal lapsed, Meek looked around for another outlet and Caroline's main competitor, Radio London, came into view.

By mid 1966 record hyping was rife on this station. Meek could buy spins

RADIO CAROLINE North

at £5 a time, and his occasional handouts of £200 could purchase chart placing on the Big L Fab 40. Crates of whisky were sent to the station, and much wining and dining of DJs was the norm for Meek's promotion effort. At the end of an evening of conviviality, wads of notes would be handed over hidden inside a newspaper. Orgy parties were also arranged at Meek's flat. Prostitutes of either gender were hired to entertain the Radio London staff.

The MV Galaxy home to the hugely successful Radio London.

ON THE AIR 1964-1968

SOME CLASSICS PLAYED ON RADIO CAROLINE NORTH - AND PROBABLY NOWHERE ELSE!

DOUBLE SHOT OF MY BABYS LOVE - *Swinging Medallions*
YOUNGER GIRL - *The Critters*
TRAIN TO RAINBOW CITY - *The Pyramids*
WEDDING IN PEYTON PLACE - *The Pyramids*
RED RUBBER BALL - *The Cyrcle*
FOOLING AROUND - *Chris Montez*
POORSIDE OF TOWN - *Johnny Rivers*
TIME SELLER - *Spencer Davis*
GRANNY TAKES A TRIP - *Purple Gang*
FLOWERS FOR MY FRIENDS - *Joyce's Angels*
OFF TO DUBLIN IN THE GREEN - *Go Lucky Four*
MY MONKEY IS A JUNKIE - *Peter Lincoln*
LINGERING ON - *Peter Law*
SENTIMENTAL SONGS - *Freddy Davies*
5 LITTLE FINGERS - *Frankie McBride*
OLD RIVERS - *Walter Brennan*
THE HURT WON'T GO AWAY - *Karen Young*
OVER THE WALL WE GO - *Oscar*
YOU'RE BREAKING MY HEART - *Keely Smith*
REMEMBER ME I'M THE ONE WHO LOVES YOU - *Dean Martin*
DIGGING MY POTATOES - *Heinz*
YOU WERE ON MY MIND - *We Five*
LONESOME ROAD - *The Wonder Who*
I'M A NUT - *Leroy Pullins*
OH NO NOT MY BABY - *Maxine Brown*
WE'RE ALL GOIN TO THE SEASIDE - *Raymond Froggatt*
PLEASE STAY - *The Crying Shames*
BEANS IN MY EARS - *The Serindipidy Singers*

RADIO CAROLINE North

Philip Solomon initially wanted to start a Caroline record label, but distributors were wary of a conflict between this and the majors. So in Autumn 1966 Solomon formed his own label, Major Minor releasing a mixture of Irish singers together with the licensing of well chosen independent American tracks. The first two releases on 25 November were by the O'Brien Brothers and Odin's People. Other artists who gained much airplay on Caroline included the Dubliners, David McWilliams, Freddie "Parrot Face" Davies - plus more contemporary sounds from Johnny Nash, the Isley Brothers, Kim Weston, Tommy James and the Shondells, Crazy Elephant and the controversial No. 1 "Je T'Aime" by Jane Birkin and Serge Gainsbourg. Airplay on Caroline South was particularly successful because good reception throughout Europe produced many Top 10 hits in France, Germany, Holland and Belgium. One notable plug song was the classic Otis Redding track, Sittin' on the Dock of the Bay. Solomon also placed the first white artist on the Stax label - Lena Zavaroni.

The biggest promotion campaign for any artist was launched for David McWilliams with his classic "The Days of Pearly Spencer" but even with constant exposure on Caroline the record failed to sell. A few years after this, one of Ronan O'Rahilly's minders, 6' 6" Jimmy Houlaghan, took over the management of David McWilliams - a deal McWilliams came to regret as he was swindled out of music royalties amounting to £2 million.

For the DJs of course the plug records were a real irritation. Each week Solomon produced a grid listing songs to be played at specific times. During 1967 the Major Minor label released over 100 singles - including songs by the Grumbleweeds, produced by Alan Freeman - previously director of the Tony Hancock albums, the Radio Ham and the Blood Donor.

Most other songs were produced and published by Scott - Solomon Prods. Ltd. Another publishing offshoot was Tee Pee Music (named after Tommy Scott and Phil Solomon). Staff at the Major Minor office monitored all these plug tracks and any deviation from the list was a serious offence. Solomon claims to have fired Tony Blackburn for omitting play list tracks on the breakfast show. He also says he ordered Ronan O'Rahilly out of the building - only allowing him back on condition he stopped interfering with the music choice.

Against this background Jerry Leighton returned from Caroline House in Spring 1966 and again became Senior DJ on Caroline North. Earlier music controller Ken Evans had also left head office on the 20th January.

ON THE AIR 1964-1968

SECRET MEETING

Since the start of offshore broadcasting to the UK in 1964, the Labour Government had threatened legislation to ban the stations. The Conservatives, champions of free enterprise, always showed a positive interest in the pirates and hinted that, when next in government, they would introduce land based commercial radio. Just weeks before the 1966 general election, Phil Solomon, the new head of Radio Caroline, was invited to a secret lunch at the Bucks Club in London's West End. His hosts were Conservatives Edward Heath and Lord Lampton. They asked for Solomon's help in placing election commercials for the Conservatives on both Caroline ships. In return Solomon would be offered preferential treatment when legalised commercial radio was eventually allowed by the Tories. Phil Solomon stuck to his side of the bargain and tapes were duly delivered and broadcast. In spite of the adverts the Conservatives did not win the election - and some years later when land based radio was proposed, the Conservatives denied any knowledge of the meeting and the agreement. Solomon even wanted to invest in London's new Capital Radio but Richard Attenborough mysteriously blocked the offer.

Back on Caroline North, Graham Webb came up from the South ship in July to set up a news service. His news team included John Aston and Dave Williams - and the major headline this month was that on the 28 July 1966, Edward Short presented the MOA to parliament.

News Room

RADIO CAROLINE North

WEDDING CELEBRATIONS

Also in the summer of 1966 Ray Teret left the station - to concentrate on running the Ugli Bug Boutique in Douglas with his sister Janet, who on 20th September married Mick Luvzit, live on air with an audience of 4 million.

On the launch, Che Sara, the bridal party was delayed by bad weather and the ceremony began three hours and two minutes later than planned.
Mick Luvzit was married under his real name, William James Brown and the service was conducted by Captain Martin Gips, 31, under Panamanian law. The best man was DJ Jerry Leighton. The ship's bell rang to start the ceremony and acting as "secretary - interpreter" was first mate, Michael Jackson who read out the stipulations of the Act in Spanish.
Janet wore white hipster trousers, with a short jacket, bare midriff, knee

ON THE AIR 1964-1968

length lace coat, bouffant veil - but no shoes. Mick meanwhile was wearing high-heeled shoes. After the seven-minute ceremony, a toast in Dutch cider was drunk to the newly-weds ending a radio first on that day, Tuesday 20th September 1966.

Government papers from the Public Records Office reveal concern about the validity of this marriage. The Daily Mirror and the Sun had asked for legal clarification and the Panamanian Consulate General stated quite firmly that a marriage at sea on their registered ship was legal.

British legal officials also knew of the couple's plan to have a second ceremony in a Manchester Register Office and asked -

"If they wish to be described as "Previously went through a form of marriage on board SS Caroline on 20th Sept" can we stop them? Both parties appear to have an English background and are presumably domicile. So I think we can say that the form of marriage is not a marriage that is known to have been null and void. However the place of marriage may give rise to difficulty since the ship may have a registered name different from Radio Caroline North. The British Consul in Panama will be approached to accept a certificate under Article 18 of the Foreign Marriage Order 1964".

TRANSMITTER POWER

There were plans to increase the Northern transmitter output to 50kw. A large crate had been stored in the forward hold just beneath the antenna, which, according to Martin Kayne, probably contained an RF amplifier capable of adding wattage to the original two 10kw sets. Fuel consumption, however, would have increased for the extra generator power and an improved mast would have been required. With the threat of legislation, development plans were put on hold. The device was later removed from Caroline North and installed in the Mi Amigo for its re-launch in September 1972.

At the end of September 1966 Graham Webb returned to Australia and Jim Murphy headed back to Texas. From that point the Country music show was hosted by Don Allen, who increased

RADIO CAROLINE North

the listenership and also produced an hour-long country show for the South ship. At this time the North News service was run by Dave Williams and Nick Bailey.

A new transmission frequency was tested during October and November and from Sunday 18th December 1966 the station moved permanently from 199 to 259 metres.

1967

During February 1967 newspapers reported payola aboard the ships. Philip Solomon had introduced a scheme in January for record companies to buy plays for their songs. The normal deal was £100 a week (minimum 3 weeks) for repeated plugs. If the songs entered the charts it was play listed at no charge, but if it failed to make any impression, it was dropped. It was a disc by Cliff Bennett and the Rebel Rousers that was at the centre of the storm. "I'll take Good Care of You" was dropped after two weeks of play with the band naturally upset by the decision. Record companies protested about the system but conveniently omitted to remind readers that they had been purchasing airtime on Radio Luxembourg since the 1930s.

In March 1967, the threat of legislation was growing and the DJ turnover increased. Paul Kramer arrived in March staying only two weeks before joining Radio 270 off Scarborough. Jerry King took his place on Caroline. Also joining was former Head DJ on Caroline South, Dave Lee Travis. A difference of opinion with the London management had forced DLT to leave - but he was quickly re-hired by the northern station.

Dave Lee Travis

ON THE AIR 1964-1968

Welcome support for the ships came from members of the House of Lords. Lord Denham put up a spirited fight for their continuation until the BBC alternative programme was available nationwide -

"Listeners to pirate radio had swollen, according to one opinion poll, to 20 million and during the months of Government inaction they had begun to look on pirate broadcast as a permanent part of their lives. The alternatives for the government were to draw listeners away from the pirates by providing the audience with what they like and doing it better than at present. The second alternative was to draw advertisers away by offering legal land based radio stations with better financial terms free from the taint of evading the law."

Lord Sorensen meanwhile was determined that the pirates last not one day longer than necessary. His views show vividly the vast cultural gulf between legislatures and voters -

"I understand that these emanations greatly stimulate and gratify the younger generation, and even a considerable number of those whose youth is receding or had receded. Hence this is described as "pop" or popular - although in this instance popular is not synonymous with plebeian, because I understand it embraces a number of patrician aural appetites."

Lord Denham revealed some current rumours in the same debate in April 1967. He pointed out that Radio Luxembourg would recapture its huge audience once the pirates had gone - and Luxembourg was commercial radio outside the control of the British Parliament. He also said that two high-powered stations were ready to start from the Iberian peninsula. Radio Andorra had already made test broadcasts, and a foreign backer of one pirate station (most probably Allen Crawford) had negotiated an agreement with Spain's Europe One to carry English programmes. Another rumour said that an American religious organisation was prepared to finance "pop" programmes to Britain from a ship in a foreign country that did not have similar legislation to the MOA Bill, manned by nationals of that country. All they wanted was to broadcast one religious talk to this country each day.

In a later debate on May 1st Lord Denham was critical of the Government who he said could and should have introduced the Bill as soon as the European agreement was signed on the 22nd January 1965.

RADIO CAROLINE North

The bill, he said, would then have sunk the pirates without trace.
Back on Caroline North Bob Stewart left in late June, with Mick Luvzit departing late July being replaced by Dee Harrison from New Brighton.
The gloom continued when Edward Short, Postmaster General, spoke these chilling words about the new Radio One -

"The purpose of the new BBC music programme is not to be a substitute for the pirates. It is not possible under the law to put out the kind of programmes the pirates are broadcasting. Radio One would have to accept restrictions on broadcast time devoted to gramophone records. Legitimate broadcasts could not ignore copyright. The new programme will provide for a wider range of music than the pirates. The BBC is convinced Radio One will be popular."

On Tuesday 8th August, the same day that Caroline's London office was closed and the furniture shipped to Amsterdam, members of the Manx government were recalled from their summer recess for an emergency debate on the station's future. Also that day Jerry Leighton presented his final Breakfast show. Newsreader Nick Bailey also took his final tender back to Ramsey. Both said they were leaving to avoid going to jail.

Over half of the Manx parliament demanded the recall of Tynwald to protest against rule from Whitehall. Members sought help from the UN against Westminster's imposition of legislation to the Island against the wishes of the Manx Parliament - which they saw as "incompatible with the freedom of a self-governing democracy."

Edward Short, the Postmaster General, also approached the Irish government to bring in the MOA. Luckily Phil Solomon had a high-ranking contact in the Irish parliament, and the Bill was quietly consigned to the bottom of the legislation list.

On Sunday 13th August, Dave Lee Travis, Tony Prince and newsman Dave Williams, the only Britons left aboard, decided to quit - they told the press *"it is not worth the risk of prosecution."*
The Ramsey tender was due to leave for the ship at 3.45pm on Monday the 14th. A lively group of fans gathered to await the return of DLT and Tony

Prince. They also saw for the first time a new team of replacement DJs - Mark Sloane and Martin Kayne.

Going back to Radio Caroline North. Off the Isle of Man.... Dee Harrison (left), Mark Sloane and Don Allan (in black blazer).

Both had been on other ships and were now taking the cause of freedom to its extreme. The Act threatened prison or massive fines.

Mark Sloane and Martin Kayne were previously with Radio 355, the short-lived successor to the easy listening station Britain Radio. Mark began his

RADIO CAROLINE North

career on KING Radio, which soon became Radio 390. A short spell on Caroline South was followed by a less happy time at Radio Antilles. Returning to the UK he joined Radio 355 in its final months.

Martin Kayne, inspired by DJ Brian Matthews, debuted on Radio Essex in January 1966, where on £12 a week, he also read the news and prepared meals for fellow DJs and crew on the Knock John Fort. In 1967 Martin climbed aboard Radio 355 until its closure on 5th August. He then smartly hotfooted it around to Caroline House for an audition and was offered a job as newsman on the Northern ship at £20 a week - a cut of £5 on his 355 salary.

On the afternoon of Monday 14th August DLT presented the afternoon show until 6pm after which Dave Williams read his final news bulletin, and together with Tony Prince, the trio - all wearing black armbands - boarded the final tender back to Ramsey. Returning from shore leave was Dee Harrison who was back on air after the 6pm news. Don Allen, Jimmy Gordon and Wally Meehan also returned from shore leave together with new recruits Martin Kayne and Mark Sloane, who had been hired by long serving Caroline Programme Director Chris Moore. The tender arrived at 4.15pm - just in time for the new boys to hear the sad farewells from the established DJs. Statements to journalists expressed defiance.

Mark Sloane "I am fighting for free radio and free speech."

Martin Kayne - "I don't know for sure what I will do but I believe in what we are now doing."

Dee Harrison - "I am prepared to come ashore and be arrested and go to the Court of Human Rights in Strasbourg."

They arrived on board the radio ship where Tony Prince and DLT were hosting their final show. Out of respect for this sad occasion, the new recruits stayed in the lounge.

DLT's show until 6pm was followed by Dave Williams' final news bulletin and minutes after this the tender returned. Dee Harrison then presented a three-hour show, followed by Don Allen until closedown at 1am.

Because of delays in applying the act to the Isle of Man, Caroline North was perfectly legal for longer than the other broadcasting ships. Instead of August the 14th, the Manx MOA didn't come into force until Friday 1st September.

The last British journalist legally aboard the ship was Robert Kelly who sailed out to Caroline on Saturday 26th August. It was a journey he said he wished never to repeat as the tiny fishing vessel tossed about from side to side.

"The 35-minute trip and the dramatic transfer served to impress on me the unappreciated hazards that have been the DJs lot since they arrived three years ago. Getting off the Offshore 3 was like being on a bucking bronco - the swell sometimes leaving a gap of yards between us and the rust-pitted side of Caroline. For the DJs it was just routine, but for me one trip was certainly enough."

One of the Caroline crew, chief engineer Hank Koning from Holland met Margaret Gale in Ramsey where they were later married. After a time in Holland they returned to Ramsey where, for many years, Hank was an Auxiliary Coastguard where he looked out to sea and remembered the old times.

Considerable press coverage was guaranteed when Ronan O'Rahilly paid a defiant visit to the island on August 30th, the day before the act applied to the Isle of Man. Less happy with the visit was DJ Martin Kayne, who O'Rahilly described as sounding like an announcer on the BBC Home Service. It took Martin several days to shake off the depression.

Once the act came in, police officials warned supply crews they would be prosecuted for visiting the ship. Radio Caroline had lost her lifeline and the alternative was a long journey into southern Ireland. Aboard Caroline, costs were trimmed by reducing the crew - now consisting of the Captain, a cook, steward and a marine engineer. A radio engineer still switched on the two 10kw transmitters at 5.30am. A 15-minute tape at 5.45 was the prelude to live programmes from 6am to 8pm after the MOA.

With just days to go Caroline North fielded a team for a charity soccer match in Onchan Stadium. Sadly the poor standard of play was noticeable when Mark Sloane was reprimanded by the referee for running with the ball in his hands.

Don Allen was now in charge as Programme Director, but was saddened to see most of the established Caroline North jocks leave, having previously expressed a determination to defy the legislation. For the new recruits it was an unsettling time. Being from the south they had not normally listened to the station and to suddenly find themselves replacing hugely popular DJs was daunting for the first few days. Listener reaction though was overwhelming in their praise for continuation of their favourite station.

Advertisements carried by Caroline North on August 15th included Coca Cola, Consulate cigarettes and Schick razor blades. All these companies denied placing the ads and explained they had cancelled all commercials as

RADIO CAROLINE North

We did not buy ads, say firms

RADIO CAROLINE claimed last night that international firms had booked £300,000-worth of advertising on its two pop-pirate stations.

The claim brought swift retorts from Beecham, Horlicks and Nestles, whose products are still being advertised on Caroline North and South, the only pirate ships not silenced by new legis-

By CLIFFORD DAVIS

from some for a few charitable organisations.

"The ads are for international products and the contracts were arranged before the new Act came into force." He added: "The money has come from international funds of the firms."

Advertisers abandoned Caroline in the months after the M.O.A.

from midnight on 14th August - quite why when the North station was not yet illegal was a question not posed by southern journalists. One perfectly acceptable ad was for the Bachelors summer show at the Futurist Theatre, Scarborough. It was placed by the firm presenting the show, P. P. Music Ltd, headed by a certain Phil Solomon, who explained he had not authorised the commercial and now had no connection with Radio Caroline.

Meanwhile a Granada TV crew planned to board the Southern ship to film a profile of Ronan O'Rahilly for the World in Action series. The TV crew had chartered a 260-ton Dutch ship, the Jacomina and once they had filmed aboard Caroline they would then head to Flushing, Holland. By this method they could not be accused of aiding a pirate ship. This was their second attempt. Their first try was on Monday 14th when they sailed out of Felixstowe on the Ross Dainty. These plans were thwarted by legal arguments. The second attempt on Tuesday was successful and the World In Action, O'Rahilly File went out on ITV at 8.30 on Monday 25 September.

On Wednesday 17th August a Government delegation travelled from the Isle of Man to meet Home Office Minister, Alice Bacon. Speaker of the House, Charles Kerruish and Secretary to the House Edward Kermeen wished to protest about the new law but came back feeling badly let down.

"The Home Office was only according English county status to the Island and was adopting a casual attitude to our interests."

ON THE AIR 1964-1968

Matters then turned to Manx Radio. Charles Kerruish stated that nothing in the agreement precluded an increase in power to improve reception in the UK.

"It is inhibited purely because successive administrations in the UK have decreed that sound broadcasts with commercial advertisements should not be accessible to the British public."

DJ Wally Meehan didn't last too long on board. He left on Sunday 27th August. Dee Harrison also decided to quit after some six weeks back on board and shortly afterwards Mark Sloane left after being reported landing at Dundalk by a Daily Mirror reporter.

A few weeks after the MOA, the DJs joked that they were planning to test the act by swimming ashore. Coastguards were so concerned they sent out a lifeboat to warn of the dangers of sea temperature and currents.

Also affected by the act were suppliers from the island. Harry Maddrell, skipper of the Essex Girl, was later First Mate on the Offshore 3, another supply boat from Holland. Almost daily the small boat sailed out to Caroline with supplies of food, fuel and water. The crew of the Essex Girl was asked to provide the service by boat owner George Cowley of the firm, Heron and Brearly. If any member of the Caroline crew was ill then the boat would immediately set off to bring him back to the mainland.

Ripley Torn joined to give Don Allen a month's shore leave and later in September another recruit, Jason Wolfe, joined the isolated ship.

In October programmes were extended to midnight with the arrival of Freddy Beare (the Caroline South newsreader Ross Brown). November saw the arrival of the enigmatic Lord Charles Brown. DJ recruitment was now handled from the Major Minor record label office - where Phil Solomon's personal assistant was Joan Thirkettle - later to be a TV news reporter for ITN.

DJs were paid via Ireland, and most had a bank account in Dublin. This enabled them to avoid UK tax, until the money was brought back to England. Martin Kayne then argued with the tax inspectors that because he had been denied residency in the UK he was entitled not to pay tax on any freelance earnings. A reasonable point but sadly the government wants it every way and HM Tax department still demanded their cut.

One of the first companies to attempt to launch pirate radio in Britain went into liquidation on 21st September 1967. CBC (Plays), formed in 1960, had as directors, Kitty Black, Allan Crawford and Major Oliver Smedley. They later invested heavily in Radio Atlanta. CBC folded owing £11,816 but with assets of only £4,864. Allan Crawford revealed he had personally lost £30,000 on the venture.

RADIO CAROLINE North

CHAPTER FOUR

ON THE BEAUTIFUL ISLE OF MAN

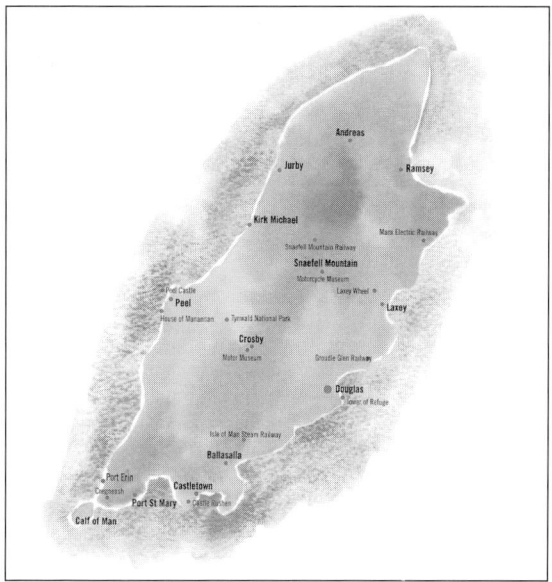

The Isle of Man is a Crown Dependency - it's part of the UK, but not totally. For example it sets its own tax rates, it has no VAT, it isn't part of the EEC and most importantly it has its own parliament, the Tynald, that has autonomy on lawmaking. Corporal punishment, like whipping with the birch, remained legal on the Isle of Man much longer than in the rest of the UK. This ability to stand at an arm's length from Britain has encouraged a fiercely independent outlook on life. It therefore came as a shock when the British government insisted that the Marine Offences Act should apply also to the Isle of Man.

This probably shouldn't have surprised the Island because the British had for decades thwarted the Manxmen's urge to broadcast to a wider audience. From the days when Radio Luxembourg was scooping up the majority audience in the UK, the Isle of Man had campaigned for a powerful radio transmitter. As early as 1930 the Island requested the asset but this was always denied. In 1959 Tynwald authorised a 100kw transmitter to broadcast to the

RADIO CAROLINE North

UK. Unfortunately the Isle of Man had signed up to the Wireless Telegraphy Act 1949 and still required permission from the British government.

Once it was known that Caroline would sail north in 1964, the British government finally allowed the opening of a local commercial station on the Island. Manx Radio opened just prior to Caroline's appearance but suffered from low VHF power and poor reception. Threats were made to increase the Manx power and to claim a Medium Wave frequency but once again Westminster stalled and essentially handed the audience to Radio Caroline. In recent years a new bid to produce programmes from the island has come from a consortium given the chance to broadcast on 279 Long Wave. The recent fight has again been long and arduous but the station seems likely to come on air this year - possibly starting with test transmissions paying tribute to Radio Caroline.

Ban on 'pirate' angers the Manx Speaker

The Isle of Man read the riot act unsuccessfully to the British Government yesterday in hopes of saving Caroline North from the law banning pirate radio stations.

Mr Charles Kerruish, Speaker of the House of Keys, said last night on his return from talks at the Home Office that relations with Britain were now worse than they had ever been in the past 100 years.

He said that first steps towards attaining associated status with Britain would be taken when Miss Alice Bacon, Minister of State at the Home Office, visits the Isle of Man next month.

"I would think that the Isle of Man must now seek more independence by means of associated status within the Commonwealth which would give full domestic control with the right to opt for full independence."

Mr Kerruish said he could foresee a demand for associate status rather like that in the Caribbean. "This would give the islanders the right of independence if they so desired. If they had associate status with the United Kingdom we would not be subjected to the treatment we have had the past two months. The fact that we are a small community does not worry us. We have a unique Commonwealth background."

Mr Kerruish gave warning that the Common Market was likely to be the next issue raised with the British Government. "In the past we have always had the right to opt out. But I think we will have no choice if the UK goes in. To a small offshore island equalisation of taxes would be a fatal thing."

Mr Kerruish was speaking at the island's airport on his way home from a meeting with Miss Bacon at the Home Office, where the Isle of Man deputation learned that the British law banning pirate radio stations would have to be applied to the Isle of Man, and that the Order in Council applying the Act to the island would come into force on September 1.

He called the order "entirely unacceptable to the Isle of Man," and said he felt most Manx people were in sympathy with Radio Caroline (which has a ship four miles off the island).

Sir Peter Stallard, Lieutenant-Governor of Man, led a deputation to the Home Office yesterday. He came away after over an hour's talk with Miss Alice Bacon, Minister of State, without even the small gain of delaying the Order in Council until the result of the island's appeal to the Commonwealth Secretariat is known — probably in about a month.

Never in 200 years of association had Britain behaved in this way towards the island—"not even in time of war," said Mr Kerruish.

THE BEAUTIFUL ISLE OF MAN

Back in 1967 the Isle of Man had to contemplate the might of Westminster power. September 1st was described as "Black Friday, one of the most significant day in Manx history" - the day that the Mother Country forced unwanted legislation on the island. Top UK officials flew into Ronaldsway to persuade the Manx of the argument. While very sympathetic to the cause their hands, sadly, were tied by international telecommunications regulations. The UK government was unable to offer the island a new and powerful radio station without European permission. Neither could they allow Radio Caroline to continue as this also contravened the same regulations.

In spite of this brave battle, Tynwald realised that they had to acquiesce, and perhaps win a later battle. The Isle of Man did though win an extra two weeks for Radio Caroline North. The Queen was away and unable to sign the papers of Council, so although the Marine Offences Act came in force on Monday 14th August 1967 - the order binding the Isle of Man was not applied until midnight on 31st August. The southern ships of Radio London and Radio Caroline could have earned an extra fortnight by sailing to the island, but pessimistic voices were already foreseeing a lack of advertising and a slow lingering end.

Radio London had tried to engineer a system of broadcasting from Morocco, via the radio ship but the terms of the Act forbade UK advertisers using the ship's offshore transmitter. Only the two Caroline ships remained defiant. How long they could last - and under what conditions?

The government had time on its side. National newspapers like the Daily Mail were unsure of the legislation's scope and decided to omit the programme guide to Caroline.

And listeners were about to be subjected to the massive advertising hype launching BBC Radio One. The focus shifted from the pioneer sea-borne broadcasters to the new stars of the less than "wonderful" national station.

CAROLINE AND THE DAILY MAIL

THE Daily Mail is discontinuing publication of Radio Caroline programmes because this is illegal under the new Act. Penalties range from a maximum fine of £400 to two years' jail or both.

RADIO CAROLINE North

IEE NEWS 15th August 1967

The Marine etc Broadcasting (Offences) Act 1967

How it may affect you

Pirate Radio Stations operating off our coasts may, of course, be said to broadcast the type of entertainment enjoyed by a large number of listeners.

On the other hand, they can, and do, cause serious interference with stations already operating on internationally agreed wavelengths, not only in this country but abroad. Protests have come from all over Europe. They may also jam ship's radio and interfere with distress signals, shipping forecasts, gale warnings and other essential messages.

Action by Parliament

To deal with this situation Parliament passed the Marine etc Broadcasting (Offences) Act, which came into force on August 15, 1967. The full provisions of the Act may be studied by applying for further information at Her Majesty's Stationery Office. The following is a condensation.

The Act

It is an offence under the Act to participate in any way in the activities of pirate radio stations or ships. Briefly:

Apparatus: (1) operating or assisting in the operation of the broadcast apparatus (2) carrying or agreeing to carry the broadcast apparatus in a ship, or (3) supplying, maintaining, installing or repairing the apparatus.

Supplying: Carrying people or goods to and from such stations or ships, provisioning (food, etc.), delivering any other item required or the engaging of crew.

Broadcasts: Taking part in any broadcast from pirate radio stations as an announcer or performer; or in any other capacity.

Advertising: Finally, it is illegal to advertise by means of broadcasting from these stations, to create or supply any material (including scripts, tapes or other recordings) for such broadcasts; or to invite anyone else to do so.

The Penalties

The maximum penalties for all these offences are the same: TWO YEARS imprisonment or a fine to be determined by the Court, or both.

The Popular Music Programme

None of this is to ignore the fact that there are audiences for all kinds of popular music. And the new service to be provided by the B.B.C. from 30th September, 1967, will, the Government believe, meet the needs of these audiences.

CHAPTER FIVE

LIFE AFTER THE MOA - THE FINAL SIX MONTHS

For the new DJs the first job was to learn how to operate the sound desk. All were thrown into the hot seat the next day. Martin Kayne began his hourly news bulletins live at 7am, while Mark Sloane presented the afternoon show, with Dee Harrison on the evening shift 6 - 8pm.

The radio ship was serviced for the last time from Ramsey on 31st August when she took on fresh provisions, fuel and 70 tons of water. At midnight Don Allen hosted a defiant two-hour show to prove to listeners that Caroline meant business and was not to be beaten. From then on the station was to be totally isolated from her friends, fans and trades people just a few miles away.

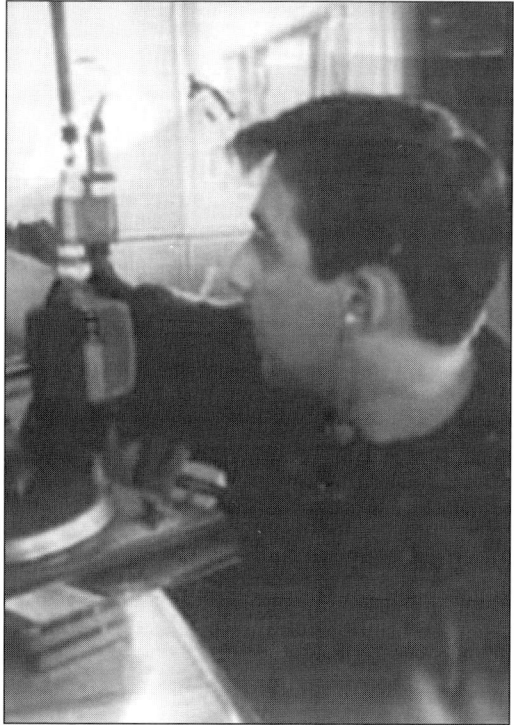

Defiant Don Allen

RADIO CAROLINE North

ENDURANCE

Liaison with the ship was via a cover company, "Record Productions" with an office in Grafton Street, Dublin. Here George Hare would organise supplies and mail services. Senior DJ Don Allen received instructions from Phil Solomon about ads and plug records. Solomon was now in charge of Caroline from his Major Minor office in London- although he avoided any publicity that would have linked him with the station. All fan mail went via the Amsterdam office, resulting in lengthy delays and a heightened sense of isolation for the presenters. The sea journey from Ramsey had been a quick 35 minutes. Now the DJs had to endure a 10 to 12 hour gruelling trip 75 miles to Dundalk aboard the converted inshore fishing vessel, Offshore 3. Ironically the Dutch tender crew often visited the Isle of Man and had no problems. The first MOA applied only to British citizens

Martin Kayne recalls the endurance test, *" With gales, an overloaded vessel and sometimes fog, with no radar, it was a miracle no one was killed. Each time I came off I vowed never to go back, but it was an adventure, so I always did. Just after the MOA we were without any supply boat for 6 weeks. I was on Caroline for 9 weeks before I came ashore. Don Allen broke a rib when the tender became caught in a whirlpool. The stern was partly submerged, the engine room flooded and two crates of long life milk were lost over the side".*

On air the spirit of good humour remained but the DJs did wonder if they still had any listeners. No mail came through for the first six weeks - but when it did it arrived in sacks. Thousands of listeners had written to the office in Amsterdam and weeks later their pledges of loyalty were a joyful lifeline to the stranded broadcasters. Programme production and news preparation keep the on-air crew busy. In the evening spirits were kept high by a plentiful supply of beer - and there was the added pleasure of watching out for announcer Mary Winters on Border TV.

This feeling of isolation obviously led to some heartache for the DJs. After 6 weeks the first to leave was Dee Harrison. Martin Kayne then took over the 6-8 evening music show, as well as continuing his newsroom duties. When Mark Sloane left a few weeks later, Martin was given the afternoon 2-6 slot. The Daily Mirror who had knowledge of his journey from Ramsey to Dundalk had tracked down Mark. After this Mark concluded that the business was becoming too fraught with uncertainty and decided to quit.

In November Caroline's share of the listening audience between the ages of 16 and 24 was 50-50 with Radio 1, according to a National Opinion Poll published in the Daily Mail.

THE FINAL SIX MONTHS

Also in late autumn 1967 the BBC began a 12-month experiment with new local stations. The first three came on air in November and broadcast only on FM - Leicester (8/11), Sheffield (15/11) and Merseyside (22/11).

On the isolated Caroline North, chief DJ Don Allen kept up morale by involving the other presenter in the running of the station. The walls of Don's cabin were covered in pin-ups and record play lists - he created a relaxed but professional atmosphere which all DJs supported. There was never any back-biting on board even though morale did sink at times when the tender didn't arrive. Presenters found it difficult to talk about fresh things and the limited play list rapidly became tedious, especially when it largely consisted of plug records for the Major Minor label. The general programme clock from the top of the hour was a chart song followed by a plug track, then an album track or a golden oldie. This order was repeated five times in the hour. The news was recorded from the BBC and then rewritten. Local headlines were taken from Manx Radio received on an FM tuner in the Caroline record library.

Record library

Don Allen

When there was little fresh news a tape of the previous bulletin was played.

PAYOLA

Some of the plug records were appalling, but without them the station would certainly have closed in August. These paid for records provided finance for the operation. Listeners certainly did notice the songs, but when Martin Kayne read out one complaint he pointed out the alternative was.....silence. Just a week later the station was silenced forever.

RADIO CAROLINE North

Martin Kayne in full flow - egged on by Dee Harrison, Don Allen, Wally Meehan, Mark Sloane and Jimmy Gordon, 30th September 1967.

On Wednesday 28th February the tender from Dundalk arrived a few days later than expected. Two DJs were returning, Freddie Beare and new recruit, the highly experienced Roger Scott - previously with Radio 390 until its closure on 20th July 1967. Almost in desperation for some work he went round to the Major Minor Records office, also used for the Caroline organisation. Jim Hoolighan offered him a job immediately and within a few days Roger arrived at Dundalk on Saturday 24th February expecting to sail the next day. With the delay, Roger and Freddie were able to enjoy a Guinness or two in Dublin. The sea passage began Tuesday evening and they arrived off Ramsey at midday on Wednesday.

Going on shore leave that lunchtime were Martin Kayne and Jason Wolfe. For Martin this was only his third break in six months -a couple of weeks in October, December and now leave from which there would be no return.

THE FINAL SIX MONTHS

Roger Scott took over the news shift from Martin and broadcast hourly throughout the afternoon. His DJ debut was on Saturday night when he presented the 6-8pm show. If this had been a weekday, Roger would have hosted the final show on Caroline North, but on a Saturday night Don Allen took the listeners through till 10 with the Country and Western Jamboree.

No one in the whole organisation knew of a crucial meeting held in Holland on Friday afternoon, the 1st of March. Here the board of the Offshore Tender and Supply Company reviewed the build up of debts from the Caroline group. On that afternoon the fate of the ships was sealed. Strong action was needed to concentrate minds and force payment of the debts. The boats were to be hijacked and towed back to Amsterdam.

THE FINAL DAY

So Saturday 2nd March 1968 dawned just like any other day on board the MV Caroline. Jimmy Gordon and Lord Charles Brown had completed the morning shows, Don Allen hosted the lunchtime show, and promoted Freddie Beare's show from 2 till 6, followed by Roger Scott 6 to 8 and then Don would be back with his two hour C'n'W Jamboree. There was no hint of the Dutch tug moored ominously a mile away. The sound of Caroline was as carefree as was possible under her siege conditions.

The studio desk used for the last time on the C'n'W Jamboree.

After mooring in Amsterdam the ship became more and more delapidated over the next four years.

RADIO CAROLINE North

THE MUSIC ENDS

Don Allen

When Don came on again at 8 - starting with Marty Robbins - he was in top form. His theme tune, Foggy Mountain Breakdown, a 100 mph banjo solo set the mood for a traditional down home programme aimed at older listeners in the North West and Ireland. He followed the theme with a classic Hank Snow track, and then another favourite, Buck Owens with "I'm Gonna Roll out the Red Carpet", played especially for Nan Honey in Cornwall.

At 8.57pm Johnny Cash's "Ring of Fire" took us into a polka instrumental up to the 9pm time-check. The final hour on Caroline North is worth recording in detail as a tribute to the communication and production skills of Don Allen.

Flatt and Scruggs classic "Foggy Mountain Breakdown" once again kicked off the hour creating an intimate wrap around effect for the next sixty minutes. The next song, Bobby Lord's "Out Behind the Bar" was a dedication to Harold Milton, a Dx'er in Norway who had written in with a reception report. Next on the play list was the classic oldie, This Old House, in country style by the Statler Brothers. To please the Irish listeners Don then played Frankie McBride with "If I Kiss You, Would You Go Away".

Next on the turntable at 9.26 was the uptempo "Louisiana Man" by Rusty and Doug Kershaw. Don was obviously in a great mood - his choice of music matched the Jamboree feel. Two more jaunty songs came on - "Uncle Pen" from Porter Wagoner's album, "Slice of Life" followed by Faron Young and "Y'all Come". A 1957 tune, later to be revived by Ireland's Daniel O'Donnell, "My Shoes Keep Walkin Back to You" was played by Ray Price who took it to number one and kept it in the charts for 37 weeks. Don then showcased bluegrass with the lively "That Good Old Mountain Dew" from Bashful Brother Oswald. Another classic Buck Owens track, "I Love You for Ever and Ever" was then segued into Bobbie Martin's "Don't Forget I Love You".

At this point Don may well have been thinking about the stationary tug a

THE FINAL SIX MONTHS

short distance away - because he segued straight into the Sonny James song "You're the Only World I Know", a number one in November 1964. At the end of these three records Don sounded slightly unsettled - he said he'd been meditating and apologised for not saying much. But being a true professional he was determined to complete his show and at 9.53 read out a dedication for Lily Lawson in St. Helens who hadn't been feeling too well recently. Don's enthusiasm must have surely cheered her up. He played her Freddie Hart's plaintive "The Ballad of Hank William's Guitar".

By now Don was almost at the end of the show, but did manage to squeeze in one final letter from a long time listener, Jim Graham in Newry, Co. Down. After this, Don's closedown was a master class in broadcast communication.

"And Ladies and Gentlemen I'm afraid that's it for the Country and Western Jamboree this Saturday evening - with the exception of the late and great Jim Reeves."

Song - "God Be With You (till we meet again)"

"So until next Saturday evening at the same time 8 o'clock, friends and neighbours, this is Don Allen saying bye bye for now. I sincerely hope you've enjoyed the show. We'll be looking forward to hearing from you - and once again to all the many wonderful folks who've written in - very very sorry we couldn't get through all the mail tonight - cos, well there's a great bundle of it, but we'll do our best next Saturday. Certainly will be looking forward to seeing you one week from tonight and once again we'll be Rolling out the Red Carpet for another Saturday night rendition of the Don Allen Country and Western - standby let's hear it! - JAMBOREE.

Disc - Foggy Mountain Breakdown - Flatt and Scruggs.

"And once again I'd like to thank each and every one of you wonderful folks out there who've made this show as popular as it is - and will continue to do so. From the bottom of my heart once again many thanks - a very good evening to you - have yourself a wonderful weekend -get off to sleep tonight and let's hope for a sunshiny day tomorrow, alright. Good night for all -and may the good Lord take a liking to you. God Bless and we'll see you next Saturday at the same time. Bye bye for now"

"The Don Allen Country and Western Jamboree was produced in the studios of Radio Caroline North on board the good ship MV Caroline

RADIO CAROLINE North

anchored 3 and one half miles off the coast of Ramsey in the wonderful Isle of Man"
   "*Broadcasting on 259 metres in the medium wave this is Radio Caroline North, National and International, broadcasting to the Isle of Man, the United Kingdom, Ireland and Continental Europe. The time is now exactly one minute past 10 o'clock".*

Disc - Jimmy McGriff - Around Midnigh

   "*Radio Caroline North, National and International, now leaves the air, to resume broadcasting at 5.45am tomorrow morning. We broadcast from studios on board the good ship MV Caroline which is lying at anchor in international waters 3 and one half miles off the bay of Ramsey in the wonderful Isle of Man. Radio Caroline broadcasts on a frequency of 1169 kilocycles - 259 metres in the medium wave band. We sincerely hope that our programmes and products have pleased you. Speaking on behalf of the Captain, Crew and the Radio staff on board, this is Don Allen bidding you a very good night - and above all God Bless.*

The final record broadcast on Radio Caroline North 10.03 pm Saturday 2nd March 1968.

THE HIJACK

Just four hours later, at 2.03am, a loud knock awakened the crew and within seconds the MV Caroline was boarded by the crew of the Dutch tug, the Utrecht, moored a short distance away for the past 24 hours. They had instructions from the tendering company to take the ship back to an unidentified destination.

The Utrecht's Captain, Martinez Menting said, *"I don't know where I'm due to sail for. I expect further instructions once I am under way. But from the course we are setting I could be ordered to go to Ireland or the Continent".* Later a spokesman for the Coastguards added, *"There appears to be a lot of activity and we think the boat is going to Greenore on Carlingford Lough in Co.Louth".*

The crystal in the Caroline transmitter was removed to stop any communication with the outside world. Simultaneously another tug had boarded the Mi Amigo, home to Radio Caroline South and both ships were now under arrest on the high seas. Off the Isle of Man, difficulties pulling up the anchor delayed the operation and gave the opportunity to one enterprising journalist to race out to the boat to conduct the final interview with the crew and DJs.

Terry Cringle was the freelance newspaperman and had been the first journalist aboard the ship when she arrived four years earlier. Now he'd received a tip off that Caroline was about to be towed away. He persuaded local baker, Ginger Crellin to take him out in a small boat. Arriving at Caroline's gangway the Captain asked him to leave, but he did manage to snatch a brief chat with Don Allen who shouted, *"I think this is the end. We don't really know what's happening, but I don't think we're going back on the air."*

Ross Brown, a former newsreader on Caroline South was also on board the North ship during the hijack and recalls the events in much detail.

"I was on leave in Amsterdam when the word came through that the North ship was going to loose most of the DJs working there because the Manx Government had been forced to ratify the MOA. We were asked if anyone wanted to go North and not to pass up an opportunity for new adventures, I readily volunteered and within 12 hours I was on my way to Ireland. I flew to Dublin, caught a train to Dundalk and met up with the tender boat which was based there. The journey to the North Ship consisted of a dash across the open North Sea to the Western tip of the Isle of Man and then depending on the weather forecasts, we either sailed around the top or bottom of Manx,

RADIO CAROLINE North

hoping the weather stayed true to the forecast. I often took the wheel of the tender boat and while sailing merrily along I could imagine that I was a real pirate.

The North Ship was much larger than the Mi Amigo, larger cabins and much more room. We received one carton of beer and two cartons of cigarettes free along with all our meals and as much tea and coffee as you could drink. Occasionally the ship's Dutch crew would break out the Dutch gin and we would party although the ship's crew and the radio station staff did not mix very much.

MOTOWN HITS

I changed my non-deplume to Frantic Freddie Beare, with the slogan, "if you have nothing on, join the Fred Beare (thread bare) show." I worked the late evening shift 9 - 12pm. I made this basically a rocking soul/blues show (Atlantic, Tamla Motown). I also took a news-reading shift that generally consisted of monitoring the BBC, recording and rewriting their bulletins and news flashes and doing bulletins during the day. Occasionally we would get news tips from ham radio operators, who made regular contact with the ship. Don Allen was the senior DJ, he had been on the North ship for a while and was well established, and he was also very popular with his quasi-country style.

My mailbag was quite modest, maybe a couple of hundred letters each week. By comparison Don's mailbag was by far the biggest, his bag was always full I guess somewhere near 1,000 a week. Don always asked for photos from listeners and his cabin was covered from the floor up and all over the ceiling with fan photos - and some were very interesting indeed. Don was also very good at return mail, probably the best.

On board life was pretty relaxed, the DJs were generally very supportive of each other. Mixing with the Ship's crew was mostly on a personal basis. At dinner there were clear dividing lines, the crew sat on one table and the DJs on another, while for celebrations it was a free for all. There were a lot of card playing schools and dart comps played and there was a ready market in beer and cigarette swapping. Reading was also a popular past time, especially the record magazines and pop newspapers. There were occasional altercations but few that I remember in any detail. Most of these were amongst with the Dutch crew, who as you can imagine sitting on a stationary boat going nowhere was not for the adventurous sailor.

The Captain used to have to start up the engines every once in a while to keep them operational. And if the weather became really bad the Captain would have to start the motors and head the boat into the wind to lessen the

THE FINAL SIX MONTHS

effect. This was sometimes problematic because the wind and the waves were not always coordinated. When major shipping was running to shelter we often felt a little exposed sitting out in open waters. We weathered some pretty bad storms at times and once had to stretch our supplies out for six weeks. I remember one gale was so bad (Force 10) the crew geared someone up with a rope and an axe to go out on the front deck to knock the chocks out of the radio mast in case we listed beyond the safety mark.

Usually we were supplied with fresh goods and diesel fuel for the generators every one to two weeks. This also meant staff rotation, when you could get off the boat for one or two weeks leave. When the weather was favourable the ships crew would winch a large cargo net over the side and we could swim in the cold North Sea. I remember one sport engaged in was throwing Sambal laced bread balls to the sea gulls and watching them go bezerk.

The trips in the tenders could also be very interesting, I remember one night the weather was really bad and all the Dutch crew were in the cabin drinking. I was hanging onto the wheel heading east\west and we were not making much headway, even under full throttle. Sometimes the squalls were so bad we actually went backwards. And this was in the middle of the night, with little to get your bearing from. On that occasion it took us twenty-four hours to sail from Dundalk to the MV Caroline in the Bay of Ramsey.

The really big danger we all faced regularly was getting on and off the ship. You had to leap from the tender boat to the main ship. Even in calm weather it was a risky jump. In bad weather it was extremely dangerous. It was a matter of timing - you had to leap from one boat to the other just at the right time. When one boat began rising and the other falling on the waves, you had to jump. Miss the timing and you could end up crushed between the two boats or in the water or maybe just with a broken leg or foot. Seasickness was another hazard, particularly on the small round bottomed Dutch tender boats. They rocked and rolled in the slightest swell, but they were splendidly buoyant and I always felt safe on them. Once I was sea sick (on a tender trip) and I got it really bad but that seemed to settle the issue because I was never seasick again.

A couple of times I did not take my leave in the Netherlands but stayed in Ireland, toured the country and saw some of the great 'Show Bands' around at that time. I also attended a Jimi Hendrix show (with the Hollies) in the North and was introduced to the audience, which caused quite a stir.

About half the ads on the North Ship were paid for and any firm advertising usually got a good run for their money. Most of the DJs liked to make out their show was well sponsored so they would often run extra ads from

RADIO CAROLINE North

the sponsor list just to make their show seem 'busy'. I think the plug records were scheduled on a half hourly basis, something like three every half hour, I cannot be certain. I remember there were some real garbage records but generally some became quite popular and one or two became big hits like the Dubliners, the Bachelors and David McWilliams. I remember that the playing of the Phil Solomon stable of stars caused the DJs heartburn because we knew that they were paying our wages. It was also something that was very closely monitored. If you failed in meeting your scheduled records then there was hell to pay, with the threat of removal from your program and ultimately off the ship.

I am certain no one else (except maybe the captain) had any idea we were going to be taken off the air. There were no sentimental/teary farewells. Early on the Sunday morning we were boarded and the crystal taken from the transmitter so we could not go back on the air. The boarding party was armed (I saw an automatic rifle) and there was no resistance, we were basically woken up to a fait accompli. In the main dining room we discussed options but without the crystal there was no way we could get back on the air and with the boarding party being armed, it was difficult to see how we could either overcome them or force them to return the crystals. The boarding party came from a tugboat (the Utrecht) that had been dispatched to tow us to the Netherlands. They worked for the company Wijsmuller and Phil Solomon had been given twenty four hours to come up with the required outstanding payment. We understood that the reason Caroline was taken off the air was about payment to the Dutch shipping company that crewed the ship and provided the supplies. We understood from wireless contact with someone representing Phil Solomon that the UK government was making it difficult for him to get money out of the UK. By the end of the day, (Sunday) despite several encouraging radio calls we accepted our fate and the tug crew began making ready for the tow and at 6pm we set off on our final journey.

Because the ship had been in the water for several years without being serviced the boat was pretty heavily barnacle encrusted and the tow was going to be slow. The journey from the Bay of Ramsey to the Isle of Wright took two days. It was brilliant weather and I had never seen the west coast of the UK and as we were going really slowly, I was able to take it all in. Gale force winds came up as we came around the bottom of the UK and we heard that there was a Force 10 in the Channel so we spent most of one day holding off the coast of the Isle of Wright. Luckily the worst of the storm had passed quickly. During this enforced delay we did hear encouraging news

THE FINAL SIX MONTHS

Under Tow

that if a deal could be struck we would head for the old anchorage off Essex and start broadcasting. Sadly this never came and our next leg of our journey took about one and a half days and we arrived (Friday) in IJmuiden, where I think I disembarked to meet my girlfriend. The DJs were all provided with transport to the Amsterdam house and airline ticket to the UK. At the house we were told by one of Phil Solomon's accountants to be ready to return to the ship on short notice. Caroline South had arrived at Javakade, Amsterdam on Monday at 5 and later we met up with one or two of the DJs from the South, who were also waiting for news. But most of them had

RADIO CAROLINE North

already left and were not waiting around. I seem to recollect Don Allen, Jim Gordon and Jason Wolfe were amongst those who waited for news. As days became a week and our pay ceased, the accountant told us the money had dried up, the house was being closed and we were encouraged to find jobs but stay in touch.

All the time we were off the air Phil Solomon remained positive that he would get Caroline back on air. A new seaworthiness certificate had to be obtained and serious consideration was given to the repairs but the costs proved too much. The spokesman for the Tender and Supply Company, Mr Eissenloeffel, also made positive statements about the future of the boats once finance had been arranged. There were several rumours that Solomon had isolated his funding for Caroline to international organisations in Europe (apart from his own funds from profits from Major Minor records and other labels he owned or was involved with) but independent sponsorship had declined to the extent that it was no longer viable to maintain the two ships - although Ronan O'Rahilly kept up a brave face, "The ships just need servicing and will return in a few weeks."

Jim Gordon (Guy Blackmore) and I decided to try our luck in the UK. We set up a record promotion company Kandoo Promotions and with the help of some friends we got a record to promote. We were supplied with a BBC internal telephone directory and with an air of confidence we stormed them and ended up getting our record promoted heavily on the BBC. The Son of Hickory Hollers Tramp by OC Smith on CBS - went on to be a big hit. Alas our money ran out before we got any commission and because Kandoo Promotions folded there was never any payout for our great promotion job.

With dwindling resources we returned to Amsterdam and raided the Discotheque scene in Amsterdam looking for work. Guy Blackmore got a job with a club near the central railway station. It was frequented by prostitutes and Guy got on really well with them, whenever they had a client with them he would always know their favourite records and play them. I was a little more fortunate as I managed to swing a job with the Kings club located in the main entertainment area. The owner had been the doorman at the Can Can club which I had often visited during the time I was waiting to go to the North Ship. Later I left the Kings Club when I was offered a lucrative contract to work for the Hilton Hotel. I was contracted to run their up market Fietsotheque (a discotheque run in their former bicycle garage). I set up an in house radio station, broadcasting on one of the channels beamed to the hotel rooms from the Fietsotheque and for a short while it was the top club in Amsterdam. In 1969 I married Patricia my Dutch girl friend whom I had met earlier at the Can Can. Pat at the time worked for KLM and she

THE FINAL SIX MONTHS

arranged for us to travel on KLM to Australia after our honeymoon in Belgium.

As a previous staff member of 2SM in Sydney I had hoped to get a offer from them but I was told I had too much of a 'transatlantic' accent and that I needed to go to one of the smaller stations to iron out the kinks. Problem was 2SM had been taken over by a new age guru and I was not one of his boys. After doing several temporary jobs, mostly as a wine waiter I was offered a show on 2LM Lismore doing their evening program from 7 to midnight. Some months later I was offered the Breakfast program at 2KM Kempsey. I left 2KM and radio in 1970 to go back to school. To fund this move I joined the Australian Public Service and started what turned out to be a new career path".

PLANS TO RETURN

There was soon speculation that the Caroline organisation may take over Manx Radio. A few months earlier (18/1/68) the Manx government had purchased the station for £50,000. Under their ownership it was assumed on the island that this autonomy would allow a huge increase in transmitting power. Tentative talks were held but Caroline ownership never transpired. Phil Solomon says he could see no merit in the enterprise, as even with increased power, the station would still only cover the North West and not penetrate the lucrative London market.

Three months after being towed back to Holland the Dutch shipping company that arranged a refit said both ships were now complete and ready to sail. Ronan O'Rahilly had spent the same months seeing advertising agencies in Holland, but with no success. No one came to reclaim the ships, the Caroline office in Holland was closed down, and the only option was for auction. Caroline North was eventually sold on Monday 29th May 1972 for £3,150 and later broken up. Caroline South was also sold that day for £2,400, officially to be used as a radio museum, but in September she slipped out to sea to resume broadcasting for nearly 8 years. During fierce gales in March 1980 she sank, but her mast remained visible for another six years.

Over the years numerous theories have been given for the hijacking of the two boats. The most widely quoted is that the Wijsmuller Shipping company had decided that the unpaid tendering bills (around £5,000 per week) had grown too large and they decided to claim the two boats and sell them to recoup the reputed £30,000 debt.

Another theory comes from Martin Kayne. *"When the towing away came*

⚡ I WANT MY CAROLINE ⚡

Ramsey Bay home to Caroline from 1964 - 1968.

RADIO CAROLINE North

I was on shore leave, at my mother's flat in London. Officially we were not supposed to enter the UK but most of us did. I have very strong feelings about the way the two ships were snatched simultaneously at what must have been considerable expense. I believe it had more to do with government pressure on Wijsmuller Shipping rather than unpaid bills. The marine supply chain was our weak link - had I been on the other side I would have taken steps to stop it, particularly as the MOA was found not to be working effectively. The Government was clearly infuriated at the station's continued survival - and was scared this could have signalled an OK for other stations to return. The MV Caroline was quite capable of sailing under her own steam, her engine was run every Monday. I would have continued aboard as long as I was paid - and perhaps more importantly as long as the listeners wanted the service. We saw this as a long-term venture. Why would anyone throw money away by running a previously profitable concern for an extra 6 months and then pulling the plug?". After the closure of Caroline North Martin became a bingo caller and worked as a DJ in a disco bar at the Odeon Cinema, Folkestone - before joining Radio North Sea in 1971.

Another report suggested that the insurers, Lloyd's of London, had refused further cover because the boats hadn't been serviced regularly. Under the terms of the insurance, each boat should be dry docked regularly to clear the hull of barnacles and to service the engine and safety equipment. Ronan O'Rahilly confirmed neither boat had been examined for over two years. The insurance cover was scheduled to run out a week after the boats were silenced - sufficient time to take them in to Amsterdam for seaworthiness tests.

The most plausible reasons for the closure lie with Phil Solomon. Since his investment in January 1966 he had seen advertising revenue decline, mostly due to the huge success of their competitor, Radio London. Even before the MOA the cost of servicing the station was colossal. He claims the Wijsmuller company was difficult to deal with. He had tried to change the service agreement but this had been negotiated long before his arrival - Wijsmuller's had obtained the Fredericia for O'Rahilly in return for a servicing contract. Items brought to the ships were individually priced - carriage of a pint of milk for instance was charged at £2-10s.

The introduction of the MOA only increased running costs. No longer could Caroline North be serviced by the short trip from Ramsey. The cost of staffing offices in Amsterdam and Dublin also increased at the same time as advertising revenue plummeted by 90%.

Solomon had kept the ship operating at great expense with little chance of ever recouping costs, although by March ad revenue had risen 40%.

THE FINAL SIX MONTHS

O'Rahilly even suggested that they were nearing a breakeven point to cover the monthly outgoings of £20,000. Genuine adverts were interspersed with dummy ones to outwit the GPO. Record companies increasingly bought airtime to expose their artists - the companies though were careful to place contracts through their music publishing subsidiaries. Phil Solomon confirms that all the major record companies were purchasers of airtime on Caroline.

The plug records from the Major Minor label also kept the stations afloat, but sales soon diminished as the national chart was influenced by airplay on Radio One. The BBC was unlikely to play list Major Minor releases if they were featured on Caroline. Although DJs disliked many of the plug songs, DJ Johnny Walker did acknowledge their importance, *"Without the paid record plugging system we adopted, we would never have lasted as long as we did."*

Solomon's revenue flow was faltering and the prospect of major repairs to the hull of the two boats was a huge cost that would offer little chance of a financial return. The lack of insurance cover concentrated minds and although Solomon had kept the ships afloat for six months, he also realised this was a battle the government was not willing to lose. A small company against the might of Westminster could have only one winner. It was therefore time to be decisive - and the free radio dream disappeared.

Ronan O'Rahilly's belief in free radio was one shared by millions of listeners, but in reality freedom always comes at a price. In Caroline's case someone had to pay for the dream with hard cash. Without money to buy that freedom, state control and restrictions always prevail.

In place of offshore radio we were expected to be content with the BBC's watered down version of pop radio. When commercial radio was eventually allowed on shore from 1972 the mass of regulations even included the imposition on presenters of a "meaningful speech" quota. Religious and community programmes also had to be heard throughout the week. Free radio in the sense of free selection of quality music soon evolved into repetitive play lists of the most obvious. Gold stations now rotate as few as 300 tracks. The stimulating eclectic selection heard on the offshore stations has been squeezed out not only in the pursuit of corporate profit but also in the very survival of the stations that are grossly overburdened by music fees and transmitter rental costs.

Personality and the shared enjoyment of well-crafted music was the hallmark of the offshore stations. Radio Caroline North was alive with an infectious free spirit that became an inspiration. That spirit was never understood by the government and for that we'll never forgive them. The programmes

RADIO CAROLINE North

were upbeat, lively and fully in tune with the beat group culture thriving in Liverpool and Manchester. Perhaps because Caroline North had no direct competition, the station was able to offer innovative programmes like Don Allen's Country and Western Jamboree and Jim Murphy's Midnight Surf Party. Sadly at the end a total staff of 40 in the Caroline organisation battled against the might of HM Government. This Home Office statement perhaps explains the real reason why offshore, and therefore uncontrolled radio, was perceived as such a threat to the government.

"I think we have to very seriously consider the enormous disadvantages of having a vast army of people who can communicate with each other very easily".
Inevitably there could only be one winner. We lost.

That loss has only grown over the intervening years. At home we enjoyed the upbeat tempo of Radio Caroline North that undoubtedly made a genuine connection with its audience. Behind the scenes there may have been turmoil, but from our transistor we heard only the good times. We remain grateful to everyone connected with Caroline North for those long lost hours of listening pleasure.

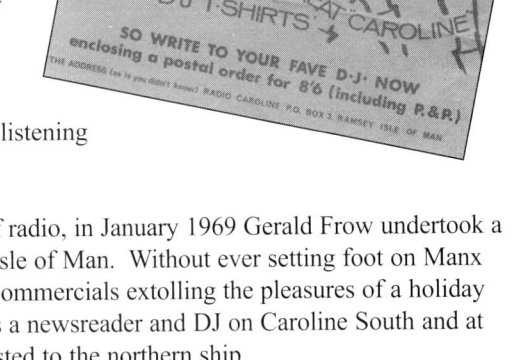

To illustrate the magic of radio, in January 1969 Gerald Frow undertook a sentimental journey to the Isle of Man. Without ever setting foot on Manx soil he wrote the Caroline commercials extolling the pleasures of a holiday break on the island. He was a newsreader and DJ on Caroline South and at one point was due to be posted to the northern ship.

"It is only now that I have been able to make it. I must say the island is as lovely as I tried to portray it on those commercials."

ACKNOWLEDGMENTS

This book could not have been produced without considerable help from the following who enthusiastically offered information and photographs.

Ross Brown
Andy Cadier
Philip Champion
Allan Crawford
Chris Edwards
Paul Graham
Graham L. Hall
Jane Harte
Barrie Johnston
Esther de Jong
John Knight
Hans Knot

Hank Koning
Henk Kruize
Peter Madison
Svenn Martinsen
John Richardson
John Roberts
Paul Rusling
Philip Solomon
Kenny Tosh
Dave West
Colin Wilkins

RADIO CAROLINE North

R.I.P.

Don Allen joined Manx Radio in March 1969. He later went back to sea on RNI. In 1975 he moved from the Isle of Man to live in Leeds. Also in the seventies he hosted a country music show on BBC Radio Merseyside. In Leeds he was employed as a cable inspector and engineer for printers, A.J.Arnold. He also presented DJ shows at the Bier Keller in Belgrave Street, Leeds. He remained in the city until January 1981, when marital problems - and the offer of work on Robbie Dale's Sunshine Radio, Dublin led him to Ireland. Later he worked for six years with Midlands Radio in Tullamore where he presented the hugely popular daily show, My Kind of Country. After feeling unwell for a short while he died in June 1995.

THE BIG wide WONDERFUL WORLD OF DAFFY DON ALLEN

SECRETARY.- Mrs. Norah E. Swallow, 5, Pundles, Bradshaw, Halifax, Yorkshire.

Go Commercial - The Friendly Station with a difference...

Manx Radio

Douglas Head, Douglas, Isle of Man
Telephone - DOUGLAS 3277
STD 0624-3277

music and information 7 am - 7 pm daily
188 & 232 m MW.   89 & 91.2 mz VHF.

Your Friendly Hosts are:-

★ **DON ALLEN:** the smooth-voiced popular Chief Announcer keen on Country-style sounds. Lots of Radio experience, and lots of fans.

★ **GEORGE FERGUSON:** the "fun-loving one" — pop is his style of music. Lives fast, drives fast, talks fast. Changes cars as often as he changes his mind.

★ **LOUISE QUIRK:** glamour behind the mike : pretty-looking, sweet-sounding hostess of Children's programme, Women's News, and her own special style of sweet music.

★ **PETER KNEALE:** on the ball with all the latest Sports News including on-the-spot commentaries of the T.T. Races. Hosts a weekly one-hour Irish Music programme. Football fan, following the progress of Manchester United.

★ **BILL CHRISP:** the good-lookin', nattily-dressed host on the Jazz programme every week. Joins Louise on Kiddies Klub-Saturday mornings. Has a crazy sense of humour-that's Bill.

★ **JOHN HUGHES:** with velvet voice-the lady's choice. Also a fast car fan. Likes smart clothes, all types of music and meeting people.

Why not Join the Official MANX RADIO FAN CLUB

Honorary Members include Top Name Stars:-
ROY ORBISON - SACHA DISTEL - THE BEACH BOYS
VIOLET (Ena Sharples) CARSON, and many, many more.
WRITE NOW FOR DETAILS!!

Daffy Don Allen
IS ALIVE & WELL
AT
Manx Radio
232 METRES MEDIUM WAVE

WE LOVE COUNTRY MUSIC
AND BRITAIN'S TOP COUNTRY D.J.
DAFFY DON ALLEN
MANX RADIO 232 METRES

SUNDAY FOOTBALL - PRESENTATION DANCE
First time in Blackpool + Personal appearance of
Manx & Ex-Radio Caroline "Country & Western" D.J.
'DAFFY' DON ALLEN
FRIDAY, 28th MAY, 1971
★ **TOWER BALLROOM** ★
BLACKPOOL
TICKETS **FIFTY** PENCE
(75 pence at the door)
8 p.m. to 2 a.m.

RADIO CAROLINE North

R.I.P.

Allan Crawford returned to the UK in the late 1970's where he continued his interest in music by writing a stage musical, "Greenhorns on the Moon". He lost a lot of money after an involvement with Scientology, but always remained optimistic about future success. A brokerage deal to lend money to the Whitlam government in Australia floundered and after an abortive deal in oil finance, Allan retired to live in north Wales where he died in December 1999.

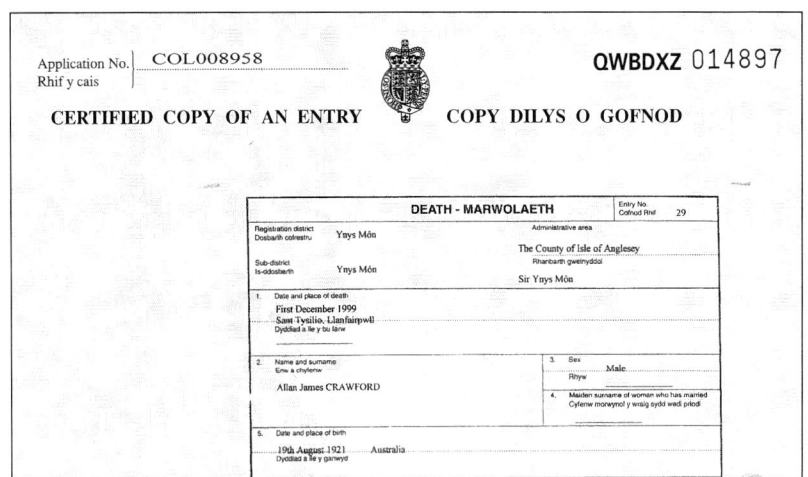

POSTSCRIPT

After his Caroline episode Philip Solomon returned to music publishing but later sold all his interests to concentrate of the management of artists and painters - a job that now takes him around the world. In 1980 he ventured back into broadcasting by financing Dublin's Sunshine Radio.

Ronan O'Rahilly is rumoured to still play snooker at the Chelsea Club, but keeps a low profile and remains out of the media. He has yet to write his memoirs.

RECOMMENDED READING

The Radio Nord Story
Prospero's Wireless by Myles Eckersley
Pop Go the Pirates by Keith Skues
Wonderful Radio London by Chris Elliot
Offshore Echos Magazine
Selling the Sixties by Robert Chapman
Fascinating web sites like the Pirate Radio Hall of Fame, Radio London, Radio 270, northernstar.no and Offshore Broadcasters all offer a wealth of information about this enduring era.

RADIO 270

LIFE ON THE
OCEAAN WAVES
an update.

Since writing the story of Radio 270 in 2002, I have been delighted to receive memories and extra information from DJs and listeners. Here are some of their fascinating stories.

Allen Ives, one of the early DJs recruited by Don Robinson, recalls the pre-transmission days.

"*As a 17 year old it was all a great adventure. I was a DJ at Tiffany's, Shaftesbury Avenue, London and had been approached by a lady from Commentators Ltd. This led to an interview in an Oxford Street tearoom with Don Robinson and Roger Gale. Having been offered a job, together- er with Bob Dewing, we arrived in Scarborough mid-March. We stayed at a pub near the harbour and helped prepare the ship - for me this con- sisted mostly of painting the hull. At that stage you'd have thought we might have been put through our paces in the studio, or at least been trained in its operation. Sadly not! Having successfully run a company in my latter years, I'd rate the organizational skills at 270 as between zero and one out of ten. On board the crew was a father and son from Holland, and the cook was a Yorkshire chap. Roger Gale was in charge of programming, and he ran this as if we were still at school, rather like a school Prefect. During March I remember going out with Paul Burnett and meeting two Yorkshire girls. As a dare and in a very drunken state I climbed the mast. As it was low tide, the ship was resting on the mud at a funny angle. Put me off heights for life. I wasn't on the boat when she sailed out so I missed the storm and the mast being chopped down. Later we all met for meeting in Don Robinson's office where he said we'd be on half pay until repairs had been completed. I oddly volun- teered to be on no pay, but was still not invited back.*"

Phil Champion kept a diary of events on the ship and says the autumn of 1966 was the best ever from 270. In February a DJ named Steve Taylor joined the station for a short time, as did Roly Roland - for one Sunday

Radio 270 An Update

afternoon show and the following day as newsreader! Phil also noted Ben Toney's second stint on the ship. Ben, former Programme Director with Radio London, had been a consultant for Radio 270 in the early days. Then in May 1967 he returned for a week as a broadcaster presenting two daily shows, 1200-1500 and 2300-2400. His news reading skills were put to the test by British pronunciation. Phil recalls a news story concerning the town of Reading. Ben fell into the trap of thinking it was the same as "reading" a book. Also around May/June 1967 Rusty Allen brought in a new roster of just three DJs on station each doing two shows a day. The DJs were Mike Hayes/Ross Randell (6-9am and 3-6.30pm) Mike Baron/Rusty Allen (9-12 and 7-10pm) and Paul Kramer/Bob Synder (12-3pm and 10-1am).

Bob Snyder made his 270 debut on April 3rd 1967 - and he describes his time with the station as rather stressful.

" The small size of the boat made life hard. Even a moderate sea caused problems. The tilt of the ship interfered with the generators that sometimes made the records run slow. Wilf Proudfoot was the kind of guy who had occasional flashes of genius - interspersed with long periods of ineptitude. In the time I was there I noticed how he ran the station as an extension of his own personality. On my afternoon show he'd often come out and forced himself on the air where he'd ramble on for a couple of hours non-stop. He also offered DJs a chance to come on the station - and some of the raw recruits were so bad, that the rest of us felt this dragged down the station's professionalism. Also in the final months he legitimised payola by accepting payments to promote a dreadful record by David Hamilton. We had to play it once an hour. Later I did hear Proudfoot was never paid for this - which makes the experience rather surreal.

The ship often went into Bridlington harbour at night. On one occasion I went for a stroll around the town after we'd berthed at 1am. I came back and two policemen were sat in the crew room supping tea. They'd come on board just for a bit of warmth and a look around. Our engineer, Keith saw them and went white. He realized the transmitter was still switched on!

I left the station at the end of July and missed the glory of being on air at the end. Why did I leave? It was the lousy conditions really and also the way Mark West was taken off air. Proudfoot heard that Mark was going to Radio Scotland and a tender was sent out immediately to remove Mark from the station. Also I recall Brendan Power being fired as well. Then there was the episode of searching the DJs as they left the ship. Proudfoot thought we were pinching the records. In fact we were throwing them overboard, they were so bad.

My resignation was over the air. I said I'd like to be taken off by the next

Radio 270 An Update

available tender. Yes I did use the words "Get me off this rust bucket". I was doing the late evening show and to my amazement the tender arrived at midnight.

Ed Moreno had also left shortly before me - and another memory I have is of meeting Rusty Allen in 1971 at the House of Commons. He was a guest of Wilf Proudfoot but our meeting was a little frosty to say the least.

These were days I'll never forget. I will always be grateful to Wilf for giving me a chance. I went on to Radio Antilles, then back to the UK with Piccadilly, Beacon and Radio Trent - plus 20 years in Canadian radio. But I have to say, those pirate days were the most exciting."

In the latter weeks before enforced closure extra news staff were recruited - local lads, Jeff Jones and Albert Clough on one shift, and on the other Phil Hayton and Julian Hewitt. An extra DJ Richard Andrews was on board for one week in June hosting 12-3pm and 11-12 midnight. Guy Hamilton also returned for a week to host 12-3pm and 10-1am. Newsman Julian Hewitt also presented a few late shows.

For its final week the station went 24 hours, and because Mike Hayes, Mike Baron and Paul Kramer couldn't return to the ship because of bad weather, Ross Randell did four shows. For the last couple of days he hosted 12.45am until 9am, 4- 6.30pm, 9-midnight and then again 12.45 to 9am. Starting one show he said, *" I don't know what the hell I'm going to do".*

North Yorkshire farmer, Tim Jackson, a founding shareholder of 270, later invested in the North East ILR station, Radio Tees. Tim died in 2002.

Solicitor Anthony Rylands, also a shareholder in 270, had his diplomatic skills put to good use as personnel officer for the enterprise. He recalls sailing out to the ship with Wilf Proudfoot to try and soothe some very seasick and mutinous DJs.

Mike Barraclough's father was the manager of the National Westminster bank, Whitby, where the £40,000 pounds investment was processed to purchase two operating companies in Honduras. Later Mike saw the ship moored in Whitby harbour every day on his way to school and was even given a guided tour one Sunday when he met Ronan O'Rahilly who was hoping to buy the ship as a replacement for Caroline.

Dave Baynes remembers the ads for Proudfoot's supermarket - which included the helpful line - "and the doors open by themselves." Memories flooded back about the news from "Radio 270....Action Central." Dave also recalls a piece in the York newspaper, dated late August 67, about Rusty Allen appearing in Scarborough court on a minor charge.

Of course after August 14th listeners could no longer enjoy the super hit

Radio 270 An Update

sound of 270, complete with catchphrases like Mike Hayes' - "Byesy Bye", Roger Keen's "I'll smash your face in", Bob Snyder's openings - "Hi, people", Boots Bowman's "You're coming on strong, you can't go wrong", Ross Randall's "Ladies and gentlemen, boys and girls, kittens and tigers", Hal Yorke's "Hello pals - it's Hal's..show" and Andy Kirk's "lovvvvveerrrrly". We miss them all.

Keep those memories coming about 270 and Caroline North!
e mail Rad270uk@yahoo.co.uk

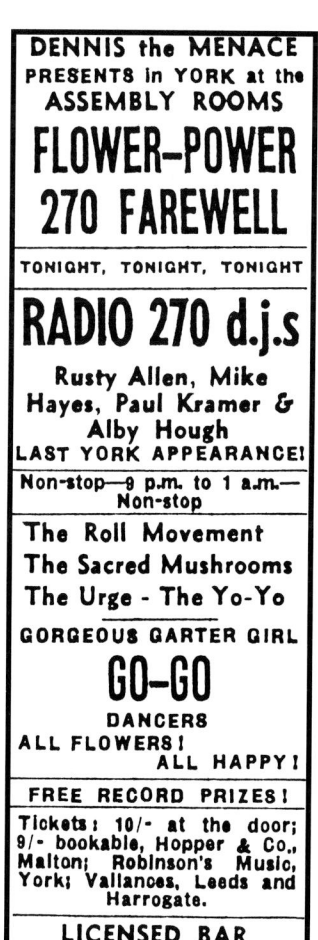

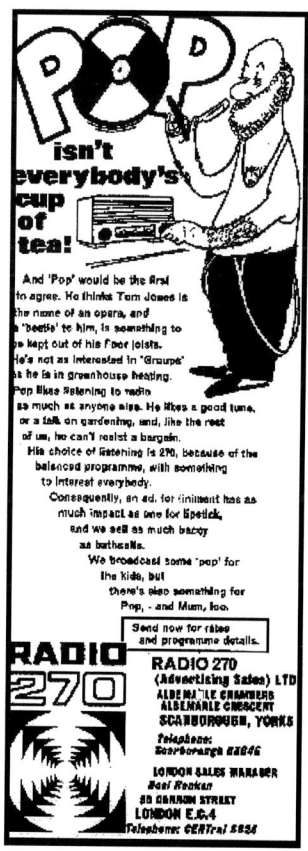

RADIO CAROLINE North

ABOUT THE AUTHOR

Sadly too young to have worked aboard the offshore stations, the author has always been fascinated by music and radio.

He began his career with the BBC in the early seventies as a cameraman working on such diverse programmes as Top of the Pops, Panorama and Jackanory. He learnt his radio craft at BBC Radio London, and after a short time as cameraman on the Old Grey Whistle Test he came north to Yorkshire Television.

After a chance meeting with Keith Skues in the YTV bar he was offered freelance shows at Radio Hallam in Sheffield. Other commercial stations he has broadcast on include Pennine Radio, Radio Tees, Radio Aire, and Magic 828.

He started presenting country shows on the BBC, first at Radio Humberside, followed by BBC Radio York where he can be heard presenting "Hot Country" every Saturday evening 7pm to 10pm. BBC Radios Leeds, Sheffield and Humberside also broadcast the show.

Back in television he was a Continuity Announcer for Yorkshire, Tyne Tees, Granada and Border for fourteen years.

Between 1984 and 1992 he ran the Castle Cinema in Pickering and since 1994 has owned the Wetherby Film Theatre.

His numerous books include two on the history of Roller Coasters and seven on Yorkshire cinemas and theatres. Recently he has completed books on West Yorkshire, Ilkley, Selby and Yorkshire for the Francis Frith Collection.In the past few years he has also written two more new titles, The history of Radio 270, and also Batley Variety Club.